KICKSTARTING YOUR ACADEMIC CAREER

KICKSTARTING YOUR ACADEMIC CAREER

Skills to Succeed in the Social Sciences

Robert L. Ostergard, Jr., and Stacy B. Fisher

UNIVERSITY OF TORONTO PRESS

www.utppublishing.com

Library and Archives Canada Cataloguing in Publication
Ostergard, Robert L., author
Kickstarting your academic career : skills to succeed in the social sciences / Robert L. Ostergard, Jr., and Stacy B. Fisher.

Includes index.
Issued in print and electronic formats.

ISBN 978-1-4426-3561-6 (paperback).—ISBN 978-1-4426-3562-3 (hardback).
—ISBN 978-1-4426-3563-0 (html).—ISBN 978-1-4426-3564-7 (pdf).

1. College students—Life skills guides. 2. College student orientation. 3. College freshmen—Life skills guides. 4. Study skills. 5. Education, Higher—Handbooks, manuals, etc. 6. College environment. 7. Social sciences—Study and teaching. I. Gordon Fisher, Stacy B., 1965-, author II. Title.

LB2343.3.O88 2017   378.1'98   C2016-904688-5
                                              C2016-904689-3

We welcome comments and suggestions regarding any aspect of our publications—please feel free to contact us at news@utphighereducation.com or visit our Internet site at www.utppublishing.com.

North America
5201 Dufferin Street
North York, Ontario, Canada, M3H 5T8

UK, Ireland, and continental Europe
NBN International
Estover Road, Plymouth, PL6 7PY, UK
ORDERS PHONE: 44 (0) 1752 202301

2250 Military Road
Tonawanda, New York, USA, 14150

ORDERS FAX: 44 (0) 1752 202333
ORDERS E-MAIL: enquiries@nbninternational.com

ORDERS PHONE: 1-800-565-9523
ORDERS FAX: 1-800-221-9985
ORDERS E-MAIL: utpbooks@utpress.utoronto.ca

The University of Toronto Press acknowledges the financial support for its publishing activities of the Government of Canada through the Canada Book Fund.

Printed in the United States of America.

For both of us, this book is dedicated to the thousands of students who have had to endure our constant nagging about the ideas and concepts we have put into this book.

From Robert: This book is specifically dedicated to my Dad, one of the funniest guys I have ever known, and the Pastafarian God, the Flying Spaghetti Monster, without whose divine wisdom this book would not have been possible. Oh, and my two cats Eubank-Kitty Meow-Meow and Hobbes-Kitty Meow-Meow (of the socialite and royal Meow-Meow Clan dating back to ancient Egypt), both of whom erased substantial portions of this manuscript while I was writing.

From Stacy: This book is dedicated to my wonderful husband, Todd, without whose divine wisdom this book would have been possible, but it was much more fun to write with him by my side. Love you, honey!

CONTENTS

ACKNOWLEDGMENTS

We will always be indebted and grateful to Mark Thompson, Editor, Higher Education Division at UTP, for approaching us to write this book. We deeply appreciate his support and belief in the project (along with his ability to overlook how we have never met a deadline during the production process). Mark moved up at UTP (congratulations!) or perhaps he just didn't want to deal with us anymore. His successor, Mat Buntin, stepped in and did an amazing job in bringing this project to completion. We ignored—um ... failed to meet—his deadlines as well.

We also want to thank Eric Herzik, Chair of the Department of Political Science at the University of Nevada, Reno, for emphasizing and rewarding undergraduate teaching, even while being at a research university.

We want to thank our students in the PSC 231 and 403J classes (fall semester 2014) for their insight and ideas on the initial concepts of this book. Their feedback helped shape our thinking in many parts of this reference guide. We also want to thank members of the Facebook Political Science Group, particularly Matthew Wilson, Rachel Bitecofer (who inspired our Google chapter), Christine Pappas, Frank Cohen, Mary Durfee (who helped inspire our research Zen sections), Beth Posner Ginsberg, Lauren Cohen Bell, Keith Gaddie, and Cheryl Van Den Handel. All of these political scientists informed some of the major sections and ideas for this project. We also want to thank the three reviewers for their insightful comments that helped to sharpen the content of the book. Finally we want to thank Jeffrey Griffin, who provided research and manuscript assistance. His hard work helped to put the finishing touches on this project.

Of course, all errors are ours alone. Yeah, right ... we're already searching for someone to blame for the errors in the book. We've narrowed it down to an as-yet unnamed graduate student and the two cats mentioned in the dedication.

INTRODUCTION

For more than 25 years now, dramatic changes have come to education in both Canada and the United States. On the positive and interesting side, the introduction of new technology, social media, the Internet, electronic information, and data have added new tools for inquiry and insight that many of us could not have imagined while we were in school. On the negative side, education has become a hot-button political topic with students and teachers at the center of public policy debates about course content, assessment and accountability, performance indicators, and budget cuts that can push the finer details of educating students to the background.

The end result is that students often enter colleges or universities without some of the basic skills that they need (and that professors often assume they have) to be successful in class. At the same time, students do not want to ask questions because they fear "looking stupid" and "being wrong." Professors then find that they have a choice: help students acquire those basic skills or let students try to figure it out on their own. Add these problems to the fact that professors have large amounts of substantive material to cover, and these skills end up not getting the attention they deserve. Our goal in this book is to help both students and professors. We want to provide students with an easy-to-read, accessible reference book that they can use for their entire time at their college or university, while also helping professors who increasingly need to find time to help students with basic skills.

As such, this book focuses on basic skills that we, as educators, find students often need some assistance to acquire or to master. From transitioning to colleges and universities to basic research skills on the Internet and within databases, we seek to provide students a starting point upon which they can build. At the same time, we have narrowed the scope of this book to the most fundamental skills. Thus, this book is not a research methodology textbook, nor is it a social science writing textbook. These important areas have already been covered in numerous textbooks on the market. Instead, our audience here is predominantly first- and second-year students who are making the transition from high school to colleges or universities and may need a resource to help them with work and with an environment that they may not have encountered previously.

Why Am I Here? From High School to College or University

Transitioning from high school to college or university is an especially stressful period. New friends, a new city, stacks of books, large lecture halls, and maybe even a part-time job mean that you are going through a large period of adjustment. All of this is occurring without the structure of high school—no teacher to tell you they did not get your paper, no old friends that you can work with easily—and you might even be learning to cook for yourself for the first time. It is a time to have fun and to explore and to develop your interests. In other words, you are balancing many new things, but you are not alone! There are literally thousands (maybe millions) of students out there who are going through the same thing.

The problem with this balancing act is that it becomes tempting to ignore things that appear difficult. When classwork becomes daunting, it can be easy to let it go or to ignore it, hoping it will go away. The end result is that work may pile up and your first term can be a nightmare. In discussions with many of our students, we learned that students sometimes ignore assignments because they either do not know how to approach them or they underestimate the amount of time and the skill level required to complete them. Our goal here is to help students acquire skills that can speed along the process of getting work done and construct the basis for building those skills moving forward. But part of developing those skills is also taking on the responsibility for acquiring them and practicing them.

In making the transition from high school to a college or university setting, you are entering an environment where you are in charge of your education. While the tools and resources for you to be successful may be on campus, you must engage those tools and resources in order to make them work for you. Every professor will expose you to the pure educational experience—talking about big ideas, helping you learn about new ways to make the world better, opening doors into ways of thinking about problems and then solving them. In a practical sense, every professor is also providing you with the skills necessary to get you started in life after college or university. They can do all of these things for you, but only if you are prepared for it, and preparing for it means having an honest discussion with yourself about why you are at a university or college.

Everybody ultimately finds her or his answers to this question but, at the beginning, you may not know why you are here. Teachers and parents have told you that you need to continue your education, but why? Some students are here to build specific skills needed for life after college or university; for others, the pure educational experience provides a basis for figuring out what they want to do with their life. In either case, you may not know what your major is going to be, or you do but you change your mind when exposed to whole new fields of study you never heard about in high school. And, for many people, education is not just a classroom experience. Getting involved outside the classroom can be just as important as what you learn from professors and teaching assistants.

While the reasons for being here vary, you still want to get the most out of the time you are at college or university. You have worked hard to get here and may be paying a large sum of money to be sitting in the classroom. Ultimately, this experience is about you and what you hope to achieve, and being active and engaged during your time here is an important part of achieving your educational goals.

Being an active and engaged student means many things. Primary amongst these things is moving beyond providing minimum effort and toward getting the most out of every college or university experience. That means figuring out how you can improve yourself by making your work, thoughts, and ideas better in terms of their depth or their expression. Learning and building skills is a multilayered process that requires digging a bit deeper every time you engage an idea or subject. Here's an example. In your introductory classes in linguistics or anthropology, you might find that languages are disappearing, that languages go "extinct." Your professor can assert that and move along in the class. But when you actively engage that proposition, your first reaction should be to ask "Why?" Every answer to the question "Why?" begins a new layer of a complex story that eventually develops a complete picture. So, the real and interesting story begins when someone asks this important question.

Professor: "Languages are disappearing around the globe. We will now
             move onto the next section of the syllabus ..."
Student: "Wait, why are languages disappearing?"
Professor: "There is not one particular reason, but we know that there
             are a few factors. Conflict can cause the disappearance of
             languages when populations are subjugated by invading forces.
             We also know that repressive governments that want to 'unify'
             populations will mandate that only specific languages be taught.
             Globalization and the spread of industrialization have also led to
             the extinction of languages."

At this point, the professor established some broad propositions to answer the question, but the details are still not clear.

Student: "But why would repressive governments want a single language enforced?"

Professor: "Languages can be a way for people to identify with each other. If you eliminate competing languages, people have a common means to communicate and may feel the differences between groups of people disintegrate. Repressing languages also becomes one of the first steps governments use in repressing entire groups. Thus, people have a real political and economic reason for wanting to eliminate language differences. The government of the former Soviet Union engaged in this type of policy by enforcing Russian as the common language of all the Soviet people. Many people lost the ability to communicate fluently in their native languages."[1]

This short engagement has elicited a layered complexity that provides not just information about language extinction, but also gives you a line of logic and analysis about why it happens. The fact that languages disappear is not that interesting by itself. *Why* it happens provides you with incredible new insights into something that, as it turns out, is a pretty complex phenomenon. The basic skills we advocate in this book are meant to build your confidence and ability to engage this level of complexity through being active in your own education. Being active and injecting yourself into your own education can open new doors for you, your colleagues, and even your professor. But being active in a scenario like this may raise one of the greatest fears of first- and second-year students: hearing the words "you are wrong."

During your time at your college and university, there are times you are going to be wrong. You are going to get things wrong in class, you are going to get things wrong on exams, you are going to get things wrong in research, and you are going to get things wrong in building your personal life. Some professors (and significant others in your personal life) will be gentler about telling you this than others. Just accept this basic fact: being wrong is a part of learning, and every person standing in front of you (i.e., your professor) has been wrong in his or her journey to the front of that classroom. The most important part of being wrong is not that you *are* wrong, but *what you do* with the information that you are wrong. Again, you need to be active and engaged with this as a part of learning. When you are wrong, you need to make sure you understand, again, *why*. Engage your professor, your colleagues, and even outside resources to find out. If your process of learning simply stops at "I'm

....

1 Adapted from Mt. Holyoke College, "Why Do Languages Die?", http://www.mtholyoke. edu/~alvar22n/Disappearing_Languages/Cause_of_Death.html.

wrong," you have stopped building the skills needed to get the best experience from your college or university. Don't be afraid of being wrong—embrace it! Albert Einstein got things wrong on his journey to being one of the most famous scientists in history. It still seemed to work out okay for him.

How to Use This Book for Students

This book is meant to help you engage a set of skills that you will need throughout your entire college or university career. You may be a first- or second-year student receiving this book in a class. It may be the case that you use only a few pages of it for *this* particular class. But, if you use it wisely, this book will be helpful in just about every class, regardless of level or year in college or university. From walking into your first big lecture hall, to taking notes, to doing research, and even to the dreaded group project, this book is meant to provide you with a quick reference on how to get started with all of the basic skills you need as a social science student. You may be tempted to set this book aside, to consider it "optional" or to even ignore it because it is not directly related to the substantive course material. But, in doing so, you may be ignoring some great suggestions for dealing with this semester. So, how do you want to use this book?

When you attend your first day of classes, grab a cup of your favorite drink and read the syllabi to identify the required assignments for each course. In doing so, you may find that you have two group projects, a number of multiple-choice exams, and a research paper due this semester. Your first action should be to open the table of contents for this book and read the relevant sections for each type of assignment. Doing this at the beginning of the semester will serve two purposes. It will give you a quick idea about how to adapt the strategies for what you have to do during the semester. And it will serve as a reminder for you to look at these again as you engage the assignments later. Not every suggestion or idea here may work for you (we hope they do!), but you will find that they help to spur even more ideas on how you can efficiently get through your already tough semester. For third- and fourth-year students who think they have all this down—take a look at the suggestions. You may find that an old dog can be taught a few new tricks!

How to Use This Book for Professors

We know that everything we have put into this book is not how *you* might do it. Our approach is direct and, at times, stark. But our approach comes from a large number of sources and experiences, many of which we share with you.

We have drawn upon almost 40 years of experience (cumulative; we're not that old) in forming our approach to these ideas and topics. We have participated in extensive discussions with others and talked with social science professors to get their input and advice on specific topics. We surveyed and talked to first- and second-year students to see what kinds of problems and concerns they had in those first few semesters. We also talked to and surveyed third- and fourth-year students to discover what they wish they had known as first- and second-year students. Even with all of this, we are still open to adjusting and adding material in later editions (if it ever comes to that!). Contact us if you find topics your students could benefit from having in the book or to see what we are tweeting and posting to help you and your students. We can be reached on Twitter: @KickstartProf; and on Facebook: @kickstartingyouracademiccareer.

We know that not all colleges and universities are created equal. On the one hand, colleges and universities with adequate resources may already have other avenues to convey this type of information to students; it may even be the case that highly selective schools do not find many of their students needing assistance with these basic skills. On the other hand, our experience has shown us that many students have never been exposed to these skills, and more and more students can use a refresher even if they learned them previously. For instance, we have talked with students who never had a librarian in their high school. How is a student supposed to learn research skills without access to a librarian? These deficits do not mean you need to dedicate all your class time to these skills. As a quick reference, this book can be assigned in the context of your class as it is already structured. Mentioning and talking about the benefits of the book on your first day and referencing it in your syllabus next to appropriate assignments will provide students with an easy reminder for them to look here for ideas that can help them succeed. No reference will be perfect, but we do hope that this book helps you to help your students succeed in your class. So, let's get started!

CHAPTER 1

WHERE TO START?
THE BASICS OF THE CLASSROOM

What to Expect from This Chapter

Going into your first college or university course can be scary. At the very least, it can be uncomfortable. In high school, you usually take classes with people you've known for a while and often have the same people in multiple classes. Also, you were continually trained about what was expected from you in class and in school more generally. When you get to college or university, the rules of the game change and expectations are not always clear. Certainly you want to be aware of the new environment and the opportunities it holds. The type of institution you have chosen to attend often dictates these opportunities. Are you at a community college or a liberal arts college where the emphasis is on teaching and close contact with students? Are you at a research university where the emphasis is on grants and research, with teaching taking a lower priority, putting distance between students and professors? Is your college or university small, allowing for better student-professor contact, or is it large, creating more barriers between you and your instructors? Your school may have 1,000 students or it may have 50,000 students. Each of these environments will provide you with different chances for learning and paths to success.

In smaller institutions, you may have a class of five people, while classes at larger institutions can have more than 500 students in attendance. In such large courses, a professor may deliver lectures while close contact and interactive learning occurs with a teaching assistant. Though the professor is responsible for the course, she or he will rely on teaching assistants to teach parts of the course and to assist in grading and managing the class. What also changes in these environments is the range of freedom you will experience, especially compared to high school.

Some professors may be diligent in getting you to turn in assignments; other professors may not care if you do homework or even if you show up to class. Thus, you need to be responsible for understanding the rules (both formal and informal) that govern behavior in each class and in your college or university as a whole. For now, our purpose is to provide some basics for understanding college and university classrooms, including the rules of the game (e.g., how to exploit all the information in your syllabus), appropriate behavior in class and when dealing with your professors, and how to take notes on readings and lectures. We will answer questions such as: How can you use the syllabus effectively? What should you expect? What are you expected to know? How are you expected to act? Keep in mind, not everything we mention here will be true at every school; however, this chapter can serve as a jumping-off point from which you can determine how things work at your particular college or university.

The Syllabus—The Rules of the Game

You cannot play a game if you do not know the rules. Well, maybe you can play (badly), but you are not going to win. The first thing you want to do in any class is to get the syllabus. The syllabus sets up the rules of the game for a classroom, and—believe it or not—professors spend quite a bit of time thinking through their syllabi because it defines how the course is going to progress. What topics are they going to cover and in how much depth? What concepts do they want their students to learn? How do they plan to judge student learning? In addition, it is (or should be) a resource that students can refer to on a regular basis to figure out where they have come from and where they are going. In this section, we talk about how to use the syllabus and why it is important to your success.

Course Management Systems

Your syllabus should note if the professor will be using an online class management system such as Canvas, Moodle, or Blackboard. If the professor is using one of these online systems, you need to learn *immediately* how to navigate it. If you have not used your institution's system previously, check with your college or university information technology or computer technology center to see if they have a class or a tutorial. If they do not, look online for videos or instructional manuals—they all have them. Take the time to learn as much as you can about how the system works, as many professors will assume that you know or will know how to use these systems. *It is your responsibility to learn them* and to utilize them for the class, and you do not want to scramble at the last moment to figure out how to submit your assignments or meet other course requirements online.

Professional Etiquette with Your Professor and Teaching Assistants

The syllabus tells you where and how you can find your instructors and teaching assistants and, often, how they prefer to be contacted. Emails, phone numbers, offices, and office hours are all listed here. Find out how your professors like to communicate and conform as best you can. It can also be useful to centralize your contact information. Create new contacts on your phone and email systems so that you have these available at your fingertips. This habit is part of recognizing you need an organizational system that compartmentalizes information for each class. Small binders or folders can keep your syllabus and coursework safe and organized for the semester.

How you communicate with your professor and teaching assistants is important. It demonstrates your professionalism and respect for them, and it creates an impression on them (and anyone else that you contact). If you can, use an email address that you obtain through your college's or university's email system. This option is generally much more professional and easier for everyone involved. It is also the email that professors and teaching assistants will use to find you in the college or university system. Besides, do you want to send your professors, assistants, or even a potential employer an email ID that begins with "skunkfarts" on Yahoo or Hotmail?

While email is available to you 24/7, professors and teaching assistants are not on call around the clock. They have personal lives and many non-teaching related pressures on their time. Read in the syllabi the best ways to contact your instructors. Be realistic about the response times. If you email your professor at 9 P.M. and have not heard back from them before class at 9 A.M., do not be upset that the professor has not responded. It is best to think of their job as nine to five (although it's not) and give them at least 24 hours to respond to questions or concerns. We often tell students that if they have not heard back in 48 hours, to email (politely) again because some emails do get lost in the ether. But find out your professor's preferences. Keep in mind that your professor may want to meet with you in person or talk with you on the phone to discuss a particular issue that you brought up in an email. Some issues are better communicated directly so there are no misunderstandings, while some issues are just too long to explain by email. Work with your professor to identify options for communication.

It may also be the case that a phone call is not the best way to contact your professor, though this varies. Some professors do not spend much time in their offices or may be unavailable even when they are present. Many faculty members do their writing and research at home and have meetings in their offices with students or colleagues. In the former case they are unavailable by phone, and in the latter it may be rude for them to answer. If you do call and you reach voicemail, leave a voicemail clearly pronouncing your name, the course that you are in, why you are calling, and one or two ways to get in touch with you, even if it's by email.

Office hours are set aside solely to meet with students, and every professor teaching a class will have scheduled office hours or alternative outside class contact hours usually mandated by the rules of the college or university. These are truly the best times to discuss more complicated issues and questions or to discuss some topic of the course in more detail. Over the years, students who take advantage of office hours have become more rare. Professors understand that students' lives are busy and complicated, but you need to prioritize the importance of your coursework and your understanding of the material. You want to take advantage of office hours to interact more closely with an expert in their field. This contact can also be beneficial to you in the future. Your professor may take the opportunity to get to know you better, understand your problems in class, and even probe your ideas on how to improve the class. All this will be helpful if you come back to the professor two years later asking for a letter of recommendation for graduate school or a reference for a job. The professor can then say something more than "he did fine in my class." It is easier to remember conversations than just a face in the crowd.

Try to get to office hours at least once a semester for each class! If this isn't possible, try to go to office hours for courses in your major. If office hours fall during a time when you have another class, you can politely ask the professor to schedule an appointment outside of office hours, but you need to be flexible regarding availability and you should show up. You can help facilitate this by providing several times that fit your schedule. That makes it easier for the professor to find a compatible time in their schedule. If you can't make the meeting, you should email or call the professor as soon as you know; this will open that time for other students or other tasks the professor needs to accomplish.

Regardless of how you interact with your professors or teaching assistants, always remain respectful. Call them by their preferred title (Doctor or Professor, not "hey"). If you do not know if your professor has a doctorate (and, therefore, is a doctor), the fallback of "Professor" is always safe. It is best to not call them Mr. or Ms. Each professor with a PhD has earned a credential and a title that goes with that credential. So, start there if you are not certain what to call your PhD instructor. Your teaching assistants can be referred to as "Mr." or "Ms." unless they have another way they prefer you address them. Your college or university is a professional environment, and professionalism requires that you call someone by his or her correct title. If your professors or teaching assistants invite you to call them by their first name, by all means feel free to do so; just don't assume that all your professors will want to be addressed in this manner. It is important to remember

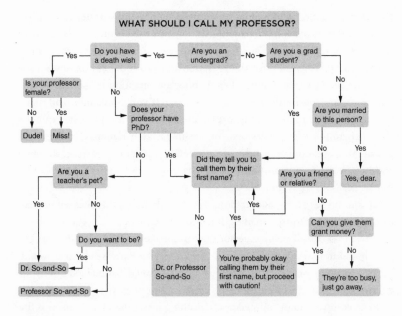

FIGURE 1.1
Reproduced by permission, Andrea Eidinger, "What Should I Call My Professor?" http://www.unwrittenhistories.com/what-should-i-call-my-professor.

that you are in a *professional environment*. It's true that you may develop a close working relationship with your professor or assistants. You may even develop a life-long friendship, but you should not assume that every professor or teaching assistant is your BFF the minute you step into his or her classroom.

When communicating with your professors, make requests, not demands, and do so politely. Many professors we know have experienced student demands or have been confronted with the comment "I pay your salary…." There is no surer way to raise the ire of anyone than to be disrespectful in your communication. So, carefully read your emails before you hit the "send" button and do not write emails while you are upset; once that email is sent, you can rarely get it back. If you are upset, open your word processing program and type out your anger, saying every nasty, awful thing you want to say. Get a good night's sleep and then see if that is what you want to say to your professor or colleagues. Civility and respect will go a long way in most situations in life, but that is especially true in dealing with your professors while in college or university.

A few more words on etiquette are warranted. Professors will establish rules for the class, and you should abide by them. Asking the professor to break those rules means that you are asking for an advantage others may not have. For example, when you ask for a paper extension, you need to under-stand that the professor is balancing this against the requirements set forth for other students. There may be legitimate reasons for an extension, but this is a case-by-case decision for the professor, and you shouldn't be upset if the professor declines your request. Lying about any situation to gain an advan-tage with your professor is a dangerous game. If you get caught, and many students have, you risk ruining your reputation with the professor (who is also likely to tell other professors) and possibly having academic charges filed against you because this can be interpreted as a form of cheating. Be open and honest with your professors, and they will be as helpful as they can be within the bounds of the course.

If your professor makes notes available on a classroom management system or through an electronic mailing list, you will have access to those notes if you miss class. But if your professor does not make her or his notes available, you should not ask for their original notes or slides—this would give you an unfair advantage over others in the course. Notes should be obtained from your colleagues if you miss class. Ideally, get notes from more than one student so you can compare them and make sure nothing is missing. Finally, there is the perennial question asked when students miss class: "Professor, I was absent from class yesterday. Did I miss anything important?" Now, think about this ques-tion. No, really. Just think about this question. One of our standard responses has become "Not a thing. We scheduled a day to completely waste time and to draw pictures of flowers, so there's nothing you have to worry about. The daffodils came out best."

Finally, one thing you will want to keep in mind is that in a university or college environment, you will meet people from all kinds of back-grounds and from all over the world. You want to make sure you treat each of your professors with the same level of respect, regardless of gender, race, ethnicity, or national origin. If your professor speaks with an accent and you don't understand what she or he has said, just ask them to repeat it. Most professors are generally accommodating and understanding. Just be understanding, too, and put yourself in their position of having to explain a technical subject in a second language! Likewise, you should make sure that you treat your female professors with the same respect as your male professors. There is no difference between their credentials, and they both have earned the right to be in front of your classroom. Any professor might have a viewpoint that is a bit different, sometimes because of their ethnic/racial background, gender, or national origin; that is the entire point of college or university—to expose you to ideas and processes that are differ-ent and new to you.

Course Information in the Syllabus

What You Want to Get from the Syllabus
- ✓ Specific assignments and due dates
- ✓ The sequence of course topics
- ✓ How your grade is calculated and the requirements of the course
- ✓ Textbooks and other readings in the sequence of course topics

So, what is in this all-important syllabus? The syllabus outlines the rules of the class, topics to be covered, related reading and other activities you need to do, and expectations for required assignments. This is all helpful information when trying to figure out how to organize your time and effort for the semester.

The first thing you want to do is to identify when specific assignments (e.g., exams and papers) are due and put them in your calendar. Most students have a calendar on their smartphones. If you don't have a smartphone, consider an online account like Google that has a calendar or other organizational tool so that you are given reminders for these assignments. You might even put in a reminder a week or two in advance of important assignments to remind yourself to get started. Remember that few, if any, professors will chase you for assignments. If you turn in an assignment late, they are not obligated to take it and often will not do so. Late assignments create equity problems in the classroom, and most professors will not take late assignments because of that issue.

Second, see how much reading is due each week so you can identify how much time must be put aside to do that critical work. Identify exam times so that you can give yourself time to study without cramming. Doing this for all your classes helps put your semester in perspective and, perhaps, helps you avoid working on five papers in the week just before finals.

Third, are there any in-class activities you absolutely cannot miss? Make sure you note those so you do not accidentally schedule other appointments during those class periods (which you shouldn't be doing anyway, but we know how it is!).

In addition to this long-term planning, you should use the syllabus to remind you where you are in a class at any given time. You will retain so much more lecture information if you don't come into class cold. If you know the topic to be discussed (which you should because you did the reading—see below) and how it relates to other topics in the course, you have the necessary context to fully understand the material.

The most important information in the syllabus that students tend to ignore is how their grade is going to be calculated. You have to know this cold for every class. Not all assignments, exams, and so on are worth the same number of points or count toward the same percentage of your final grade. Looking at how points are allocated throughout the semester makes you aware of what the professor deems to be important and also provides you with some insight into which assignments you should spend the most time on. This is not to say that you should ignore assignments that are worth only a small percentage of your grade—these can add up, much to the consternation of students—but if you have both an exam and a paper due the same week and the exam is worth 10 per cent of your grade and the paper is worth 50 per cent, you should spend the lion's share of your time on the paper. In other words, allocate your time appropriately.

Finally, use the syllabus to find information *first* when you have questions about the class. Reread the requirements of the course to save a bit of time. No professor will be sympathetic if you simply didn't read or understand what was written in the syllabus. That is your problem, and one of your duties is to make sure you know what is required. There will be information about course policies that are usually non-negotiable. For example, what happens if you are sick during an exam? Will you need a doctor's note to retake it? If so, go to the health center to get one. Does your professor post outlines for their lectures online? If so, download them before class so it is easier to take notes. What happens if you miss class? Does your instructor take attendance? Is there a limit to the number of classes you can miss before it affects your grade? This is information that will be provided to you on the syllabus. Not knowing these rules may ultimately keep you from winning the game. Make sure you understand the conditions of the course established in the syllabus so that you have no surprises later in the term.

Large Class Dynamics

A large class is generally any course with more than 50–60 students, but some courses can be held in lecture halls holding more than 1,000 students. The sight of such a classroom reminds you that you are no longer in high school, and it can be intimidating, especially if you don't know what to expect or what is going to happen on day one. What do you do in a class where you might feel invisible to or disconnected from the professor or easily distracted by the activities of your fellow students? In this section, we discuss the strengths and weaknesses of these types of classes, how they might make you feel, and how professors feel about them, and we provide some tips to succeeding and not getting lost in the (literal) crowd.

Strengths and Weaknesses of Large Classes

For students, it can be difficult to learn in big classes, but you may find yourself in many of them, especially in the first two years of higher education. Large classes are the most efficient way to convey fundamental knowledge about a subject to students so they can qualify for higher-level classes where course-work is specialized and where students will benefit more from a smaller class size. Thus, large classes tend to be lower-division courses that introduce students from many majors and backgrounds to the rudiments of a subject. Students use these classes to "test the waters" in a new discipline or to get their first look at their major. Sometimes these classes are required for majors and some-times they meet general education requirements. Sometimes they do both! Thus, much of the information you learn relates to the history of a particular discipline or field and the concepts and terms that you must know to under-stand it at its most basic level. Compared to upper-division courses, these may not be the most exciting, but they can be some of the most important classes that you take. To use an example from the natural sciences, would you want a colleague in a chemistry laboratory if they did not have a grasp of some of the basic principles of chemistry? If large classes must be held for efficiency's sake, this is the level where they will be useful. So, while many students and professors do not always enjoy these enormous classes, they open the oppor-tunity for smaller classes when you need them—at the upper-division level.

One of the ways to overcome the inherent limitations of large classes is through "tutorial," "break-out," or "discussion" sections. These are smaller subgroups of each class that meet separately from the main group, generally one or two times per week. Such sections are relatively small (more like you have seen in high school) and are usually taught by graduate student assis-tants. While we will discuss assistants in a bit more detail later, you want to be aware that much, if not all, of the grading in large classes is done by the grad-uate assistants, teaching assistants, or tutors. It is also important to remember that these tutorials and discussion sections are where you have the opportunity to ask in-depth questions and to participate in discussions and activities that build on the knowledge the professor has conveyed in the larger lecture hall.

What to Expect in a Large Class

In many large classes, attendance is never taken simply because it takes too much time. However, some professors do take attendance in lecture halls through "clicker quizzes," where the professor asks questions and students respond with an electronic device (not all colleges or universities utilize this technology). When you answer the questions, the device will register your student information and quiz answers in an electronic file that the professor can easily download. So it is important to check the syllabus for attendance requirements in the large lecture hall. Just because the professor isn't calling your name every day doesn't mean attendance is not affecting your grade, and you should be familiar with each instructor's attendance policies (they're in the syllabus!). Likewise, take a moment one day after lecture to introduce yourself to the professor! Putting a name to a face can be one way of connecting with the professor in what is otherwise a sea of faces.

Lecturing is the most direct way to provide large numbers of students with the information needed for the course, so there is not much interaction between the professor and individual students. It is more likely that, in your large lecture, you will be sitting and taking notes while someone on a stage or platform is talking to you. Depending upon the size of the course, your instructor may even be seen on a large screen or use a microphone to be heard. Some professors try to make this an entertaining exchange, incorporating jokes, a little discussion, some visual aids, or other devices to keep students interested and involved, but this is difficult to do. Remember, while it would be nice for every big lecture to be entertaining and engaging, some of your professors may not live up to that expectation. The professor's job is to educate you about their subject and to make that information accessible to everyone in the class; being entertaining while doing that is not always their expertise (and when that's the case, it is just plain awkward when they try). That means some lectures may be lively and get you involved, while others may be dry and boring. Stay focused on your primary objective in the class: to gather information from the professor so that you can understand the subject at hand. Everything else is secondary.

Large lectures are also filled with all kinds of students with different reasons for being there. For some, it may not be their major; they are just there "to fill some requirement." For others, it is their major and they take it extremely seriously. You cannot control who is there and it is probable that students around you will do things that distract you. Modern technology, for better or worse, has made this even easier to do in large lectures. Students can text or surf the Internet; post on Facebook, Snapchat, or Instagram; or just talk to their friends. Many students may play on their laptops or phones, read the newspaper, or sleep. We won't list here all the strange things we have seen students do right in front of us while we are lecturing; suffice it to say that some of them have been extremely odd!

Students are more comfortable doing all these things in a large class because they feel anonymous. Unfortunately, people *can* hear and see what you are doing. Most large lecture halls are set up in a style that allows sound to travel quite well. The professor on stage or at the lectern can hear "quiet" conversations—much to the embarrassment of the participants. So, at a minimum, you should be aware that *we can see and hear you*. Even in a class of a thousand students, we are constantly scanning the room, and we notice which students are paying attention and which are not. Finally, something to keep in mind: everybody in the lecture hall had to work hard to get there. In many cases, they may be paying money to be there as well. Disruptive behavior on your part is unfair to your colleagues and to the professor. A few suggestions about large lecture hall etiquette may help you avoid what could be an embarrassing situation.

Large Lecture Hall Etiquette

The Do's of Large Lecture Halls
✓ Show up on time
✓ Take notes on what the professor says, what she or he writes on the boards or projectors, and anything pertaining to the syllabus or direction of the course
✓ Ask questions to clarify what you do not understand
✓ Stay home if you are sick or too tired to stay awake

Show up on time. If you are late for the class, you may need to cross in front of people who are trying to concentrate on a lecture that has already begun. Try to be the least disruptive you can be if you are coming in late. Find a seat in the lecture hall quietly so you do not disturb your colleagues.

Take notes on what the professor says, what she or he writes on the boards or projectors, and anything pertaining to the syllabus or direction of the course. If you miss something in the lecture, try to refrain from asking your neighbor or colleague while the lecture is in progress. Make a margin note to ask a colleague, the teaching assistant, or possibly the professor after class. Remember, you can always email the professor or your teaching assistant if you miss something in the lecture! You have many options for getting information you may miss, so relax a little bit and *listen* to the lecture while you take notes. You will find this a much more rewarding experience than frantically scrambling to write every word down.

Ask questions to clarify what you do not understand. If the professor takes questions during the lecture, take advantage of this and ask for clarification on points that you do not understand. While speaking up in a large lecture hall can be intimidating, think of yourself as a spokesperson for the dozens of other students who most likely have the same question. Remember that this is your education and you should want it to be as complete as possible.

Stay home if you are sick or too tired to stay awake. If you are sick, you will only make your condition worse by not resting, particularly during cold and flu season. The best thing you can do for yourself and others is stay home; you will feel better faster, and you will prevent others from contracting your illness if it is contagious. The same rules apply if you are tired and cannot stay awake during the lecture. You may think that falling asleep in the lecture is not a problem, but you are wrong. Students are not aware of what they do when they are asleep. What can happen? Snoring so loudly that the professor can hear it at the front of the class; falling out of your seat; dropping books and notepads on the floor or on top of the person seated in front of you. The worst-case scenario is when the professor stops the lecture, walks over to where you are sleeping, and hovers over you until you wake up to the laughter of the entire lecture hall. If you are too tired to be in a lecture, you should be home sleeping out of respect for your colleagues and the professor.

The Don'ts of Large Lecture Halls

* ✗ Do not leave your cell phone on during the lecture
* ✗ Do not text during the lecture
* ✗ Do not record the lecture without permission
* ✗ Do not surf the Internet while the lecture is in progress
* ✗ Do not talk during lectures
* ✗ Do not start secondary conversations
* ✗ Do not do other work in the large lecture hall
* ✗ Do not start packing up your belongings until the professor has ended the lecture

Do not leave your cell phone on during the lecture. If you must be reachable, sit near the door, put your cell phone on silent or buzz, and quietly leave the lecture hall to take your call when it comes.

Do not text during the lecture. It is obvious when you are texting on your phone and it is rude to do so. Trying to hide the phone by your side or under the table makes it even worse. If you came to a professor's office hours and all she or he did was text while you were trying to get your question answered, how would you perceive that action? You would probably immediately go to social media to complain about how rude your professor was to you. And rightfully so! At the same time, if you do go to a professor's office and are going to take notes on your phone or tablet, let the professor know so that there is no chance of misconstruing the purpose of your texting. A little communication can go a long way toward avoiding misunderstandings, and this scenario is one example of that.

Do not record the lecture without permission. The lecture the professor gives is proprietary information and it should not be recorded without his or her permission. If you have a disability that requires assistance in this way, make sure that the professor is notified through your disability resources center. In some jurisdictions, it can be illegal to record lectures and conversations without permission. Generally, your college or university student conduct code governs what you may be able to record, but it is always best to check with the professor delivering the lecture.

Do not surf the Internet while the lecture is in progress. First, the professor is going to know and may choose to single you out for reprimand. Second, it can be distracting for students around you—that funny video, the horrible email you just received, and the episode of your favorite show are all things that can be seen on your screen by other students, and it will distract their attention from the material whether they want it to or not. Besides, do you really want students you don't know reading your email and knowing what you watch? That's basically trolling without the effort!

Do not talk during lectures. If, for some reason, you really need to say something to the person next to you, make it as quiet, discreet, and fast as possible.

Do not start secondary conversations. If the professor is taking questions, do not use this as your cue to start a conversation with the person next to you. Many people will be interested in the questions and answers, and your conversation should not make it difficult for them to follow the exchange.

Do not do other work in the large lecture hall. If you have work for other courses or other things you want to do, you should not bring these into the large lecture hall. Reading for another class or studying other material is rude to the professor. The expectation in the lecture hall is that you are giving the professor your full attention. If you cannot do that, it may be best for you not to show up to the lecture. Eventually, the professor will notice your lack of attention and even call on you to address material that is being discussed. You will not be able to do so and you will find yourself embarrassed in front of the entire class.

Do not start packing up your belongings until the professor has ended the lecture. Few things are more annoying to students and to professors than when people start packing their gear while the professor is still conveying information. The information at the end of a lecture is often just as important as the first word of the lecture. If the professor keeps running over time, politely ask your teaching assistant to make the professor aware of this so that you can more easily get to your next class.

Each of these issues is generally referred to as a lecture hall disturbance and can affect the professor's ability to maintain control and decorum in such a large environment. It's not that your professor likes being a "hard ass" about rules and etiquette. She or he has a duty to provide a proper learning environment so that all students have the chance to get the best grades that they can. If students are distracting and disturbing to others in the room, that goal becomes less and less achievable. Thus, every professor may react differently to lecture hall disturbances. Some may politely ask you to refrain from engaging in the offending behavior. Others may subtly stare at you while they talk to let you know that they can hear and see you. Still others may point to you in the lecture hall, ask you to gather your belongings and leave. If you have never experienced this reaction, you will find that being reprimanded, disciplined, or asked to leave in front of 200 of your colleagues will probably be one of the most embarrassing things ever to happen to you. To be clear, the professor has every right to take any of these actions, and these experiences may negatively affect future relationships with your colleagues and professors. No one wants to do a group project or presentation with someone they have seen called out for bad behavior in another class. Similarly, you may find you need an upper-division class that is only offered by the professor who has kicked you out. In either case, do you want to be remembered as "that jackass from the intro course"?

Professors, Assistants, and the Large Lectures

There is no universal opinion about large lecture halls among students or professors. Some professors enjoy the large audience and have an amazing time putting on a good lecture. Other professors, particularly at large colleges or universities, like the distance it puts between themselves and the students. But many do not like the minimal interaction that such classes impose. Having taught a few of these classes, we can say that the experience can be a good one, but it can also isolate us from our students.

As noted elsewhere, large classes are usually taught at large colleges or universities that also produce a significant amount of research. Professors are the primary source of this research. Graduate students earn their advanced degrees by engaging in research (often with professors) as well. At some research schools, professors teach only one or two classes per term because they are required to spend large portions of their time (usually 40% or more) conducting research to advance knowledge in their area of expertise, to publish articles and books, and to train graduate students in their field. Regardless of the size of your college or university, your professors will also be required to complete some form of administrative service that helps your institution run smoothly. They do student advising, perform other forms of service in their departments and for the campus more broadly, attend conferences, review other scholars' research, serve on boards, and numerous other activities. What this means is that your professors are busy, but they still want you to get the most out of your education. Thus, graduate assistants play an important role in getting you through a course when the professor's workload does not permit them to meet the needs of every student in a large lecture.

In big classes, you will probably be expected to attend tutorials or discussion sections that are led by a teaching assistant. Most teaching assistants are working toward an advanced degree in the department in which the professor is teaching. While your teaching assistant helps in the classroom, they may also be one of the professor's doctoral students (a person working toward their PhD). The teaching assistant leads the tutorial or discussion sections and is generally responsible for grading your coursework during the semester. They serve an important role in the large lecture hall in that this person is your point of contact for the entire course. Your questions and issues in the class should be directed to the teaching assistant. That being said, if you are having an issue with your graduate or teaching assistant, you should not hesitate to make an appointment or go to your professor during office hours to make them aware of your concerns.

Students and the Large Lecture Hall

Large lecture halls can be good and bad for students because there is some freedom to make them your own experience. Some students love them because of the anonymity they feel and having the choice to attend (or not). If your tendency is more toward the slacker side than it is toward the productive side, large lectures give you plenty of freedom to follow that calling. But this freedom rarely works to a student's benefit. As a first- or second-year student, all your classes are important, and those introductory courses should serve as a grade point average buffer for more difficult classes that you will be taking in your third and fourth years.

We have seen too many of our students try to skate through their first year or so without taking grades seriously enough. As a result, many first- and second-year students find themselves on academic probation because their grade point average dropped too low. Trying to increase your average from a probationary status is one of the most difficult things a student may have to do—it takes many classes to build it up whereas it takes just one failure to drag it all the way back down. Thus, large lecture halls for students can be good if they are given the attention they require, but bad if you do not navigate them well.

With large lecture halls filled with positive and negative incentives, how do you keep interested and succeed? We offer a few suggestions that seem to work for many of our students.

As one student of ours was fond of saying, "Just suck it up!" To some degree, you have to live with the situation and make the best of it. Know the potential impacts of large classes on your academic record and motivation level, and do your best to stay in tune. Keep focused on the job at hand and keep your attention on the professor. If you do that, you will notice that they will catch your eye once in a while—in fact, you will be surprised how often this happens. This signal is an easy reminder that you are not completely inconsequential and that the lecture is a two-way interaction.

Don't go to class! (But there are strings attached to this, so read on.) If you know you cannot be focused in class, maybe you shouldn't go—at least once in a while. Not everything goes smoothly while you are in school. Maybe someone back home has gotten sick or you had a fight with your parents or you are just stressed about another project. If one day you just can't focus your attention or you didn't sleep well the night before, do not go to your large lecture class (make sure you get notes from someone else). You don't want to get into the habit of going to class but not paying attention while you are there. That habit will never serve you well. If you only go when you know you can be attentive, you are less likely to develop habits that will diminish your ability to succeed.

Avoid being anonymous! Sit toward the front of the class. Doing so does not mean that you always have to sit in the front row, but sitting in the first couple of rows limits the number of students sitting in front of you who might be doing something distracting. In addition, the students in the front rows tend to pay closer attention, so they are less likely to do something to get your attention. The professor also looks at these students more often because they are the ones making eye contact. Once again, if you feel you are being looked at and spoken to, it will be easier for you to pay attention.

Read! Do the reading before the lecture. Below we talk about why this is so important for information retention, but it also helps you remain attentive in a large class. If you have done the reading and have some intellectual connection to the topic, then, when the professor is talking, it is easier to pay attention because you have a better understanding of the material and context of the lecture. Having done the reading, you can judge more clearly what is important in the lecture and focus on that material. If you know what the professor is talking about, even in a broad sense, it is less difficult to remain attentive.

Communicate! If you are having trouble with the course material, speak immediately to the professor or teaching assistant, and do not assume you "will 'get it' later." Concepts and ideas in introductory classes tend to snowball; you need to understand previous material so what follows down the road makes sense. If you do not understand material and it begins to compound over time, you will feel increasingly less interested in the class (doomed to fail, so why bother?) and your poor performance becomes a self-fulfilling prophecy. You are more likely to succeed when you feel that you understand the material, so at the first sign of trouble, get into your assistant's or professor's office and camp out until all your questions are answered.

Smaller Classes and Tutorials, Sections, or Labs

Most students and professors prefer smaller classes. We would love all of our classes to be fewer than 25 students. There are expectations in small classes that must be met, though they differ significantly from large lecture hall classes. Smaller classes in the social sciences still usually involve a professor lecturing (hey, we love to talk!), but your role will probably be much more active. Many small classes have discussion components where you are expected to contribute to the intellectual exchange among your peers. In other words, much of what you do in a discussion section in a large class will be done during the regular period in a smaller class.

What to Expect in a Small Class

You can't run and you can't hide! In a small class, professors often know every student's name, and they know who has done the homework and reading (the ones who don't look at their shoes and mumble "Please, please, don't call on me"). Attendance may be taken more frequently and discussion of readings may occur more often than in large lecture halls. Smaller classes tend to be upper-division courses, so the requirements to complete the class are going to be more intense and demanding. All the large lecture hall etiquette points are now magnified as well—side conversations, texting, and tardiness are much more obvious to the professor or the teaching assistant.

Smaller classes also give professors the opportunity to engage students with different types of assignments and exercises. Some of these include group exercises, presentations (yes, you may have to talk in front of a group!), simulations, videos, and even guest speakers or lecturers who provide different insights into the subject at hand. Your participation in these assignments and exercises can be crucial for numerous reasons. First, actually engaging in the class assignments and exercises can make the experience much more enjoyable for you—you get the opportunity to meet people in the class and to engage with the material in a much more in-depth fashion. Second, your engagement in the exercises makes it more enriching for other students as well. Think of it this way: when you were a kid at the playground, how much more fun was it when you had others to play with, to solve puzzles, or even to get into a bit of trouble? In the same way, professors expect you to participate actively to gain a more sophisticated understanding of the material.

As we said earlier, there are going to be some different requirements and expectations in smaller classes. Let's take a look at one of the more common forms of engagement that occurs in smaller classes: discussion and participation.

Course Discussions and Participation

Discussion and participation can be one of the most interesting parts of a small course because it allows you to engage with the material in greater detail than you can in a large lecture hall. It can also be one of the most difficult requirements for students to navigate. Have I participated enough? Does it make sense? Why do I feel stupid compared to other students? These are questions most students have at one time or another. Your professor may have a rubric that clarifies what constitutes "good" participation and how much constitutes "enough" participation. We'll go through some rough guidelines to help in a moment. With regard to whether you make sense, that is what discussion is meant to discover. These discussions are not meant to embarrass students; rather they are meant to see if you have a working understanding of the material being discussed. Of course, this proposition only works if you do the reading. But if you did and you have misunderstood what you have read, this is a good chance to have that mistaken understanding fixed. You may be hesitant to speak or engage the professor in discussion because "others seem so much smarter than me." This feeling is common among students. Keep in mind that you will be in classes with all sorts of students with different backgrounds. Upper-class students (e.g., third- and fourth-year students), students majoring in the topic, and people who have experienced the subject in the "real world" can make you feel unprepared. That's okay. You shouldn't feel "stupid" or "dumb." Instead, you should engage these people and learn from them as well. The professor may not be the only person in the class that has insight into your topic. For instance, if you were in a sociology or psychology class dealing with family counseling, wouldn't insight from a student who has done an internship in family counseling be enriching for the entire class? Do not think of people who may know more at that moment as an opportunity to hide—it's an opportunity to engage and to be better in your subject! With that in mind, let's take a look at some guidelines for good discussion in the classroom.

Guidelines for Good Discussion

What Makes for Good Discussion?
✓ Do all homework and readings before class
✓ Bring your notes and books to class with you
✓ Have questions ready from the reading material
✓ Be cognizant of your own participation
✓ Don't be disagreeable, but disagree if you need to
✓ Strike a balance between quantity and quality

✓ Don't be THAT student (you're familiar with THAT student;
   keep reading!)
✓ Attending is not participating!
✓ Make comments that are based on evidence and
   well-constructed arguments

Do all homework and readings before class. The primary reason that students feel "stupid" in discussion is because they have no clue about the discussion topic. Discussions generally revolve around readings you were supposed to have done for the class, and if only one or two people have done the reading, then you are only going to hear from those one or two people.

Bring your notes and books to class with you. If you have made notes about your readings (see the discussion below about how to do this), bring them so you can refer back to them. Your notes are key to bringing up those important points the professor is going to try to get at within the discussion. Feel free to open your book during discussions to refresh your understanding of the material.

Have questions ready from the reading material. In some cases, your reading assignments are straightforward. In other cases your professor may try to tease out some complex ideas and theories. The reading may be difficult, complex, and even confusing. If you do not comprehend the material, write questions down in your notes and bring them up during discussion. These questions demonstrate you're actively thinking about the material and not just letting the readings wash over you.

Be cognizant of your own participation. You may be up to speed and really into this subject, but you find that every time you talk, you hear sighs from the back of the room. Are you starting to dominate the discussion to the exclusion of others? Your professor may regulate this by saying she would like to hear from other people. If you start to get negative reactions, back off for a couple of minutes to let others have their say. Remember, the professor has only a set amount of time and may want to get everyone to say something, so don't be offended if the professor bypasses you. You want to balance your participation and that of others in the class. Still, professors understand the enthusiasm to say something, particularly if participation is a substantial portion of your grade.

Don't be disagreeable, but disagree if you need to. The whole point of having a discussion is to bring to light facts and ideas that get us to a better understanding about a topic. Social science courses are always filled with controversy, heated debates, and alternative and strong opinions. You are never going to agree with everything you hear in a class from your peers or from your professor.

You shouldn't. You want to develop a solid understanding of the way the world works, as we understand the facts. If you are just ignoring facts because they don't conform to your view of the world, then you run the risk of weakening your position by not addressing and fixing flaws in your argument. What this all means is that you should feel free to express ideas in opposition to what people in the class are saying. Hold your ground if you are convinced of the facts and strength of your claim. It's also okay to admit that you may need to rethink part of your argument. The most important part of this type of exchange is to maintain respect for your peers, your professor, and yourself. Name-calling or belittling other's ideas (e.g., "That's just a stupid idea") will never win a debate for you and will cause you to lose respect and credibility with your peers and professors. Your exchanges should be strong, even strident, but respectful to keep the discourse friendly and accessible. It is acceptable to disagree with a professor's interpretation of an idea or theory; it is okay to ask professors where they got their information or how they came to their conclusions. It is never appropriate to disparage, belittle, or personally attack a professor (these are referred to as *ad hominem* attacks). The end result of such an exchange can range from creating a tense, disruptive environment in the class to being barred from the class at the professor's discretion.

Strike a balance between quantity and quality. Saying something just to say something shows that you are not engaged with the discussion or material. The purpose of discussion is to bring out the important material for the class and to try to work through problems and puzzles collectively. Let us give you an example. In a class on contemporary Russian government, the professor asked students to think about political tactics that the Russian president used to control his opposition. While the professor expected responses such as intimidation, cronyism, and corruption, one student proclaimed torture was a tactic being used. If there were evidence the student could cite, this would have been a fine answer. But then the student began to give a history of how the Tsarist governments going back centuries had used torture; students began rolling their eyes. He was quickly turning into THAT student.

Don't be THAT student. Who is THAT student? There are several characteristics of THAT student; each will provoke varying levels of eye-rolling from colleagues in the classroom. THAT student asks questions that aren't really questions. They want to show their knowledge without acting like a know-it-all. Their questions often start with phrases like "Isn't it true that …?" THAT student wants to lecture other students but knows that doing so directly is rude. Asking a question in this manner isn't always annoying, but if you find yourself repeatedly asking your questions like this, you may want to reconsider your approach. THAT student also tries to answer every question: Yes, professors want to hear your viewpoint and have an active discussion. However, if you raise your hand for every question, the other students in the class start to zone out, knowing that you will take care of the whole discussion if they just lay back and let you. Social scientists call this "free-riding"—contributing nothing while taking advantage of the contributions of others. When professors don't call on you, they are trying to put pressure on other students to engage the material. If this happens, hold back for a little bit and let others carry some of the weight. Otherwise, you may be in danger of being the second lecturer in the class and turning into THAT student! They also make unnecessarily long and involved comments about the material. Once again, this is usually a way to illustrate knowledge and lecture other students (and the professor). Everyone listening is aware of this. Students eventually stop listening, and the professor will try to figure out a way to stop you without embarrassing you. Thus, few will be paying attention. Did everyone need a multi-century lecture on the use of torture in Russian history? No! No! No! No, they did not!

Attending is not participating! Just because you show up doesn't mean you are entitled to get credit for participating. By simply showing up, you have fulfilled the *"mushroom requirement"*—you have not done anything more than a mushroom would if it was sitting in your seat. Professors know students are reluctant to speak up, but there are strategies for dealing with this issue. Take a look at Chapter 4, which deals with oral communication and presentations. Some of those hints will be useful to get rid of the jitters you may face in class.

Make comments that are based on evidence and well-constructed arguments. Professors enjoy seeing students take information from the lectures and notes and apply it to examples and cases. This type of participation highlights *quality over quantity.* What makes for a high quality discussion? By doing the reading, you have the requisite knowledge to make quality comments and ideas in the class. It is obvious when students participate in a course discussion without the requisite knowledge to do so well. Likewise, apply the concepts and information from the class. If you say something that someone who has not taken the class can offer, this only keeps the conversation from advancing. We want to know whether the information makes sense to you and whether you can apply it to real-world questions and situations.

Let us look at a simple example. Say you are in an introductory sociology class and the current topic is "What does it mean for a person to be 'socialized'?" You've read the chapter and listened to the lecture. If you are discussing this topic in class, then it is likely that both the professor and the author have mentioned some specific characteristics in the reading and lecture. Look back at your lecture notes or open the book to the appropriate section (this is not cheating, and professors often like to see students doing this—it implies they are trying to relate the discussion to the material). What did they say about this topic? Are there details you should be focusing on? For example, if the reading mentioned that socialization is a process of passing along customs and values, a well-constructed comment might be the following: "In the book they talk about how people acquire customs and values. So, one example of this may be in learning the national anthem in grade school." These points create a precise and appropriate comment that adds to a discussion.

In conclusion, high quality participation requires that you come to class and do the reading. Above and beyond everything we have just said about discussion and participation, there is another reason you want to do this and it is the most important. You do not want to just sit by and let life and your education pass in front of you. Take a stand! Engage in a debate! Expand your mind! You cannot experience life and education as a bystander. If you are just going to come to class to "be the 'shroom," you miss the opportunity to expand your horizons beyond anything you imagined the day you stepped onto your campus. Don't waste that opportunity.

Revisiting the Lecture

We know you are going to be busy. But small amounts of time can be valuable if you use them wisely. You should not take notes and then forget about them until it is time for the exam. If you take five or ten minutes before each class to go back over notes taken previously, you will remind yourself of the context of the information and, as we will discuss throughout this book, having a context for storing information is important to remembering it. It would be a good idea to look at your lecture notes in combination with the related reading notes to see if you can figure out how they are connected. (Because they are!)

Important Points to Remember

How to Succeed in College Courses
✓ Understand and use the syllabus
✓ Use your professors and graduate assistants as resources, but be respectful

In a Large Class
- ✓ Take actions to help you stay focused
- ✓ Be aware that your professor can see and hear you
- ✓ Do not be disruptive to those around you
- ✓ Keep up with the material and ask questions when you have them

In a Small Class
- ✓ Same as in large classes AND
- ✓ Be prepared to participate in activities and discuss the material in a constructive manner

CHAPTER 2

SO YOU THOUGHT YOU KNEW HOW TO READ? READINGS AND NOTES FOR CLASS

As we discussed in Chapter 1, the syllabus establishes the rules of the game for the course. It also outlines the sequence of topics and the readings that go with them. Your textbooks are critical to your success in a course. In conjunction with what your professor will teach, the required reading provides important insight into the ideas and concepts that you will be learning in the course. But simply reading or skimming the reading material does not lead to success. Likewise, when your professor is lecturing, what should you be writing down? Let's see how you can make your time reading and taking lecture notes a bit more productive and effective.

Textbooks

All professors have had the following complaint from students. "I've done all the reading but I'm still doing poorly on the quizzes or tests. The questions are too tricky!" When we talk with students about this, the first question we ask is "How are you studying?" Generally, students will tell us that they read the material, usually before class, and then reread it before the quiz or exam. This answer suggests that the student may not understand the difference between reading and studying. At the root of the problem is *how often* and *how* the student is reading the textbook. In this section we discuss how to read a textbook for most efficient information retention. Some of this advice comes from recent academic literature, but most comes from our experience in our own teaching and learning (yes, we still read to learn things). In our experience, students taking this advice retain more information from their reading and end up doing better on assessments. The key is to figure out the strategy that works for you and do it every time you read a textbook or any similar course material.

How Often to Read

We won't go into detail here, but there has been a considerable amount of research done on how often students read textbooks. This research has generally found that while professors want students to spread out their textbook reading so that they read for each topic before the appropriate lecture, most do their reading immediately before an exam (Clump et al., 2004). This is problematic for two reasons.

The first is that, if you wait to do all your reading until immediately before the exam, you don't have the base knowledge needed to understand and follow the lectures given throughout the semester. You may be thinking, "But I understand the lectures!" You are probably wrong. You may understand some of what is being said, but you would have a greater depth of knowledge and a more sophisticated understanding of the lecture material if you had the background information provided by the textbook. You would probably even remember the lectures better! This is especially true in introductory-level social science courses where the textbook is used to provide details and specifics about a topic while the lecture is used to explain theories of why things work the way they do. It's hard to understand the theories if you haven't even heard of the concepts that underlie them.

Second, as all students have been told, "Cramming[1] doesn't work." Trying to cover too much information at one time immediately before a test can have an effect on long-term retention of what was learned (Willingham, 2002). Only so much information can be shoveled into a single brain in one 6- or 12-hour period. You cannot remember the information from six or seven chapters of a textbook that you've read in one study session. Each chapter likely includes dozens of important terms and concepts and the relationships between those concepts. While you might be able to memorize (at least for the short term) the definitions of most of them, your college or university tests do not just focus on definitions. You will also be tested on how the concepts relate to one another and how they fit into a variety of theories and conclusions about human behavior. Remembering these relationships requires understanding—not just memorization—and understanding is better generated through study time that is spaced evenly throughout the semester.

Finally, few students cram only during the daylight hours before an exam and then get a good night's sleep. If you are a "crammer," odds are you stay up cramming most of the night before an exam. You need your sleep after studying and before an assessment so that your brain has time to organize and to structure information for maximum memory efficiency.[2] Cramming

....

1 Academics refer to this as "massed" study time as opposed to "spaced" study time.
2 A quick read by John Grohol on how sleeping helps your brain remember and organize information can be found at PsychCentral: http://psychcentral.com/blog/archives/2008/08/03/while-you-sleep-your-brain-keeps-working/.

and lack of sleep before an exam mean that the information is just floating around in your brain without any way to structure it. You will retain more information if you are able to get some sleep. Even if that means getting some catnaps along the way, sleep will rejuvenate your body and refresh your mind so you can think more clearly and retain more information. This points to a larger issue—taking time to care for yourself will make you more productive and much more capable of handling stress. Taking a walk, doing a workout or sport, and eating right can prepare you for stressful periods. Ignoring your body and mind will lead you to more bouts of illness, being prickly during periods of stress, and can even contribute to unhappiness.

How to Read and Take Notes from a Textbook

When students come into our offices wondering why they received a worse-than-expected grade although they read the material, the first thing we ask is "How did you read the textbook?" This is usually met with a confused look and the following response, "I just sat down and read it." You will probably be surprised to learn (as our past students have) that the worst ways to retain information in a book are to read the chapters linearly, from start to finish, and trying to read all the chapters for an exam at once.

There is a HUGE amount of information in the average social science textbook. As we noted above, there are terms and concepts that have to be defined and explanations for how those concepts relate to one another. There are often multiple and/or competing explanations that you need to compare. The problem with reading linearly is that you are reading all this new information without any understanding of how to organize it and, unless it is organized in a logical way, your likelihood of remembering it is extremely low. You need to provide your brain with context—a set of "bins" in which to put the new information. Then, when you read the chapter, every individual piece of information you come across has a logical place to go, from which you can retrieve it later. We also believe that having the context to put your information into helps you to better understand the relationships between concepts and why each concept is being discussed at all.

For quite a few reasons, many students today are not taught study skills that can help them with the densest of textbooks. As a result, students have picked up habits that work against them instead of for them. Before you delve into your textbooks, we think we can offer some advice showing one method to help you simplify and learn even the densest of material. We originally wrote much of this method for Wikihow ("How to Study a Textbook," http://www.wikihow.com/Study-a-Textbook), and our students have found it useful. In fact, if followed through, this method of textbook studying will actually be a time saver.

Steps to Studying a Textbook

1. For any textbook you are assigned, the first thing that you need to read is the introduction to the book. If it is a book that takes a detailed look at a particular topic, the introduction will summarize the author's argument and present an outline of the chapters. If the textbook is a general introductory text, the introduction will serve to tell you how the author is going to approach the topic.

2. Survey the organization of the textbook. First, have a look at the table of contents. See how it's organized; this may help you predict what will be covered in class and on exams. Second, look at the organization of each chapter. Most textbook authors use a system of headings and subheadings to outline the topic they plan to cover in each chapter. By reviewing these and using them to your advantage, you can approach each chapter in a systematic fashion. This is very important, so here's an example of how it is done.

Below, we have outlined the chapter of a recent book on legislative lobbying by only using the chapter title, headings, and subheadings.

Chapter Title: The Context of Legislative Lobbying

I. Types and Resources of Opposition
   a. No opposition
   b. Unorganized opposition
   c. Opposition with resources
      1. Money
      2. Membership
      3. Prestigious lobbying firm
      4. Summary of resources
   d. Sophisticated opposition
II. Types of Policy
   a. Policy change versus status quo
   b. Fiscal bills versus revenue-neutral bills
III. Stage of the policy process
   a. Drafting bills
   b. Policy committee
   c. Fiscal committee
   d. Floor
IV. Conclusion

Creating that outline took about five minutes and, without having read any actual text yet, we already have some important information. First, this chapter will be talking about how the environment (context) affects how interest groups lobby. When the author is talking about context, she is talking about three things: opposition type, policy type, and policy stage. She has also outlined the most important aspects of each. For example, there are four stages of the process she'll be looking at: drafting, policy and fiscal committees, and the floor. Now, you may not know what some of these things mean yet (e.g., what does it mean to "draft a bill," or what is "sophisticated opposition"?), but you know that those terms will be coming up and you know you will need to figure out from the reading what they mean. At the least, we know what is critical for us to understand.

3. Skip to the end first. Many textbooks offer a recap or summary of the chapter content and study questions or "food for thought" at the end of every chapter. Skipping to this part first shows you what to focus on as you read through the chapter. Then, read the entire chapter through without taking notes or doing anything else. *Just read it.* You have two objectives in doing so. The first is to get a sense of the *purpose* of the chapter. Ask yourself: what is the author trying to convey in the chapter overall? Second, how does the author build the information or argument in the chapter? When you have a mental picture of the answers to these two questions, you can then begin taking notes that will benefit you in your study for exams and in writing research papers. Don't rush this step. It can be tempting to just get done with your reading as soon as possible, but you are unlikely to retain information if you hurry through.

4. Take notes and handwrite your textbook notes. Handwriting your notes forces your brain to actually engage with the material as opposed to glossing over it or mindlessly typing the same text into the computer. Notes do not mean taking down every word verbatim. The art of note taking involves discerning what is important. The first thing to write down is the main point or argument that the author is conveying in the chapter. Do this in no more than three sentences. Then ask yourself how does the author begin to make the point? This is where the major headings and subheadings help. Under each heading are paragraphs that make up the section of the chapter. Document the topic sentences that help build the argument in the section and chapter. Don't be afraid to write in your book. Annotating a textbook by writing notes, comments, and questions in the margins can be invaluable when studying.

5. Once you have done this for the entire chapter, go back into the chapter and produce two independent lists. The first notes the major concepts and principles important to understanding the chapter. The second lists key terminology with corresponding definitions (think of this as a vocabulary list that you need to know).

6. Once you do this, you will have an entire set of notes on that chapter. If you do this routinely, when it comes time for an examination, you will

have your study guide ready to do what you need to do, which is to *study* the material. Studying means that you understand the material in the chapter and that you have memorized the key information needed to be able to show you have a mastery of that information. There is no secret or shortcut here—every new subject you take is like a new foreign language. You need to learn the terminology before you can communicate. Whether it is economics, political science, anthropology, or sociology, you need to be able to communicate in the language of the discipline. The only way to learn that language is to dive in and begin dealing with that material.

7. Once you have all your notes, you can then assemble them to form your study guide. While your friends and colleagues are scrambling to reread material the night before the exam, you just need to sit back and begin memorizing your notes for the examination. Your textbook notes along with your lecture notes are your study guides.

In addition to understanding how you want to study the textbook, there are some other textbook-related considerations.

Other Textbook-Related Considerations
✓ Keep your study area quiet and without distractions
✓ Understand that reading is not the same as studying
✓ Avoid using highlight markers
✓ Don't just skip over words you do not know

Keep your study area quiet and without distractions. In approaching a chapter, some preparation will go a long way. Put away your cell phone, do not sit at a computer, and do not allow yourself to be interrupted. We often think that we can multitask and study without full concentration, but we are actually pretty horrible at multitasking. If you are going to tackle any subject seriously, then you need to give it your full attention.

Understand that reading is not the same as studying. Sometimes students will just move their eyes along the page again and again. This results in a feeling that you don't "understand" the material. Studying is an active process: you need to be engaged, paying attention, and thinking about what you read. Simply reading implies that you are not engaged with the material; studying involves a process of taking notes, understanding how the text fits with your lecture notes, and thinking about the material.

Avoid using highlight markers. While it's tempting to break out the rainbow of highlighters when you read through a chapter, resist this temptation. Research has shown that highlighting may hamper your reading because you feel tempted to highlight every single thing you feel is important without thinking critically about the ideas presented. (Take a look at Annie Murphy Paul's article on the best and worst learning techniques here: http://ideas.time.com/2013/01/09/highlighting-is-a-waste-of-time-the-best-and-worst-learning-techniques/.)

Don't just skip over words you do not know. You are going to have to look up words. It can be tempting to simply read past words or elements you don't understand in an effort to "just get it done," but this reduces comprehension. If a dense textbook on Marxist economics has a term that you don't initially understand, don't just read on: stop what you're doing, look up the word, and understand it before continuing. What you are reading will make more sense if you understand all the words. In addition, this activity helps you build a strong vocabulary.

Once you have tried this approach, you will probably adapt it to your needs and courses. Feel free to do so. Some points work for some students, while those same points may not work for others. No matter how you adapt the system, remember the fundamental points that will keep you from distractions and help you to focus on the material instead of the other things going on around you.

Supplemental Texts and Journal Articles

In most classes there is at least one textbook and, often but not always, one or more supplementary texts. In the first two years of college or university, supplemental books usually compile a series of independent readings (e.g., reprinted articles from academic journals) or debates related to the topic at hand. These are sometimes referred to as "readings" books or "edited volumes." Students are more likely to criticize a supplemental text or book of academic journal articles when used in a class, and we think this is because they don't know how that type of book or article relates to the textbook or the rest of the course.

The textbook is assigned to provide detailed facts about the subject and to present an introduction to general theories of behavior. The readings in an edited volume or supplemental text provide examples of original research, opinion pieces, or other materials on which these theories and our general understanding of the topic has developed. A textbook tells you what we know, and the supplemental text often tells you how we know it.

In addition, the social sciences are not just about "society," "culture," or "politics." These disciplines attempt to make generalizations about human social behavior by using the scientific method. This means they generate hypotheses about how the world works, collect data, and then use the data to test the hypotheses. Many supplemental texts summarize the research that has been done to figure out how we know what we know. Others may provide you with historical documents or modern essays that explain theories or arguments in more detail. For example, if you are taking an Introduction to Anthropology class and you are studying culture and language, you might have a supplemental text that gives you examples of arguments made about how language developed. It might also have essays in which experts explain different cases of how particular languages developed and evolved.

You should always read the textbook first to get a general outline of the topic. Then read the assigned chapters in the supplemental text to see whether the arguments or findings presented support those offered in the textbook. After reading each chapter in the supplemental text, you should be able to answer the following questions:

- What argument is the author trying to make? You should be able to summarize this in two or three sentences.
- What evidence did the author provide in support of his or her argument?
- Did you find the argument and evidence compelling? Why or why not?
- How does this reading relate to course lectures and the readings in the textbook?

Luckily, you can usually answer these questions by reading a supplemental text in the same manner you read a textbook. Read the introduction and conclusion of the piece, then look at the outline of headings and subheadings, read through the material, and then take notes.

Prior to entering your college or university, you probably never read the text of an academic journal article. These articles are written by professors and other researchers on a specific topic and, in the social sciences, they are usually laid out in the format of a scientific paper or treatise. This means that they include the following: a review of other articles written by other academics on the same topic, a discussion of what the article will add to our understanding of the topic, a set of hypotheses to be tested to support their ideas, the data and statistical techniques used to test those hypotheses, and the results of their scientific endeavor. Note that each section also relates to the four questions previously mentioned. However, academic journal articles are highly structured and deserve some specific attention here. Not only will these articles be assigned in your classes, they will also form the basis of much of your research (which we will cover in Chapter 4).

Academic journal articles often follow a standard format that includes the following parts and what you might want to take away from them:

- *Abstract and Introduction:* The abstract will present an overview of the article. If the article does not have an abstract, the introduction will also typically present the overview. The introduction will also explain what the authors did in the article and why they conducted the research.

- *Research Methodology:* This section can get complicated, but essentially it tells you how the researchers tested their hypotheses or propositions. This section of the research may present historical cases or complex data analyses. If you find that you do not have the background yet to fully understand the tests the researchers used, make note of the type of tests they used and, if applicable, the type of data they used.
- *Results and Analysis (or Discussion):* The researchers will present the results of their tests here. You want to highlight the key findings in their research. Did they confirm previous studies? Did they make new insights into the topic?
- *Conclusion:* What is the larger implication of the study you just read? What does it say about the topic in your syllabus or how does it fit into your research paper?

Before tackling the entire article, first read the Abstract, Introduction, and Conclusion so that you have a sense of what the article will present. Here are a few questions that will help you focus a critical lens when tackling the full article.

- Identify the author's research question—what puzzle or question are they trying to address?
- How does the author's research question and results relate to the topic within the syllabus (or your research topic when you use the articles for research papers or projects)?
- Be critical when assessing the information. Some questions to consider when doing this are
  - Do the authors clearly define the key terms needed to understand their point?
  - Do the authors present the best way to approach the research question, or are there points that they may not have considered?
  - Do the results make sense in the context of the authors' approach?
  - Do the results seem "intuitive," or do the results buck our intuition and logic about a topic?
  - Do the authors draw appropriate conclusions from their results? Have they missed something?

Approaching articles systematically in this way will allow you to relate the article to your syllabus topic, and it will also help you develop a critical eye toward research. Just because it is in print does not mean that it is flawless. The whole point of reading research is to improve our understanding of the social world. Thus, we should approach reading and research with a critical eye toward improvement, not just toward criticism.

Note Taking in Classes

This should probably go without saying, but it is important to take notes in class. Few things surprise professors more than giving a detailed lecture and seeing students who write *nothing* down. On the opposite pole are other students who try to write down every word. Neither of these strategies works. The key thing to remember is that there is a purpose to taking notes: to understand (not just memorize) information about the topic for exams and other assessments. Keep this in mind as you sit in class writing down the information that comes from your professors. In this section we will talk about how to take notes that will help you learn the information necessary for success in class.

Preparing to Take Notes

You should do the reading before class. As we noted above, this is because it provides you with the necessary background to take in and organize all the information in the lecture. You will have a better idea of what to write down from the lecture if you've done the reading first, because you will know what can be found in the readings versus what your professor is saying in class. Likewise, you are more likely to remember information if you have some idea of how to organize it in your head. Your readings can give you a sense of how to organize the lecture information. When you have a place to put information in your memory, it is going to be easier to retrieve it later.

You should do at least five minutes of preparation before starting to take notes in class. Look over your notes from the last class period. Is the same general topic going to be covered? If so, what was discussed previously and how might this new information fit in? Is it a new topic area? Even if it is, it is not completely disconnected (or at least shouldn't be) from the rest of the class. How do you think it is going to relate? You should have some idea of this based on the reading you've done. Do you have any questions about the previous lecture that you now realize you didn't understand fully? Did you write down a word in the margins and have no idea why? Ask those questions at the beginning of class before the professor starts to give you more information. Many professors provide a few minutes at the beginning of class to deal with class administration and to go over questions from the last lecture. Use this time efficiently. Take advantage of every moment that you can to organize information and to ask questions.

What Am I Supposed to Write Down?

The Do's of Note Taking
- ✓ Do not write down everything
- ✓ Write down words that you do not know and words that you know, but do not understand how they are being used
- ✓ Write down less rather than more
- ✓ Write notes by hand—don't use a laptop
- ✓ Revisit past lecture notes before each class

For a long time, high schools, colleges, and universities taught students to take notes based on the Cornell Notes system. There are plenty of sources on how to do this; the Learning Toolbox (http://coe.jmu.edu/learningtoolbox/cornellnotes.html) has a good explanation and illustration of this system. It is efficient and it works. But Cornell Notes are more amenable to notebooks and notepads and have fallen out of favor as more students (try to) take notes with laptops. Because of this, students are now left to their own devices to figure out what works best for them. Let's see if we can provide some helpful hints and suggestions on note taking in class.

Do not write down everything! The key is to write down what is necessary to understand the topic. Your instructor often provides you with cues as to what is important. For example, he may say, "There are three theories to explain why people rebel against their government. The first is...." Just from that sentence, we can tell you what the topic of that lecture is and what you need to write down. If you are actively listening, you should have questions already. What does it mean to rebel? How are the three theories different? If done well, your notes will probably look something like this.

Why do people rebel against government?
Three theories
1. Theory 1: Name and explanation
How does it cause people to rebel?
2. Theory 2: Name and explanation
How does it cause people to rebel?
How is this different from Theory 1?
3. Theory 3: Name and explanation
How does it cause people to rebel?
How is this different from Theories 1 and 2?

Now, this is not all your professor will be saying, but this is the critical information you definitely need to know. The professor will also provide you with some examples. You should understand the basics of each example—how they illustrate the theories. They are provided to illustrate concepts that might be hard to understand if they were just defined without any context provided. You might, for example, write down "Example: Egypt, 2012 (Theory 1) and present-day Syria (Theory 2)" to remind yourself of the examples provided. Then, if you are unclear about Theory 1 or 2 when going over your notes in the future, you can look up the Egyptian revolution of 2012 or the Syrian revolution to see if they provide some details.

Sometimes your professor will go off on a tangent. No matter what students think, the professor's tangent is often (though not always) related to the topic at hand. Think about how the current discussion is related to the overall topic. If you can't figure it out, ask, so you can determine how it fits into your notes (or not). It is completely appropriate to ask a question like "Is this an example of one of the theories? If so, which one?"

Write down words that you do not know and words that you know, but do not understand how they are being used. Each academic discipline has words that they have made up (lingo or jargon) or common words that they use differently. For example, in sociology the word "consciousness" has a discipline-specific definition; if you look it up in a dictionary, you will not have the correct definition for your course. In economics, the term "rational" has a very specific meaning that has little to do with the sanity of the subject. As you hear those words, write them down so you can ask your professor when there is a break in the lecture or so you can look them up after class. We guarantee if you do not write them down, you will not remember them.

Write down less rather than more. Do not write down sentences word for word. Summarize and paraphrase, but do so accurately. You are more likely to use your notes if they are clear, concise, and well structured than if you attempt to simply transcribe the lecture. As noted above, not everything the professor mentions is critical for you to remember. If you try to remember it all, the most important information can get lost in the weeds.

How Am I Supposed to Write It Down?

Here comes the big question—should you use a computer or write your notes by hand? We know students prefer to take notes with a computer because it is faster and easier to read later. We would be tempted to use a computer if we took a class today. But research has consistently shown that taking notes by hand is better for retention and understanding than notes you take on a computer. Why might this be the case? Students who take notes on a laptop *are not actively listening.* They are not thinking about what is important to write down and why; they can type fast enough to transcribe everything the professor is saying. Students writing by hand have to be more critical about what they choose to write down, so they think more about the topic and the lecture as it is occurring.[3] While you are choosing what to write down, you are critically thinking about the material and deciding what is important and what is not. You may think to yourself, "But transcribing is great! I have every-thing and can judge what is important later." That's not true. You have every word, but you don't have the non-verbal cues that the professor has provided to illustrate the most important points. You've also missed out on an hour or more (during the lecture) that should have been dedicated to thinking about the topic. You'll still have to do that at some point and could have gotten it done during class. Using a laptop does not promote success; better notes and comprehension do.

Using pens that record lectures and allow you to find certain sections of the lectures easily (e.g. LiveScribe) can force you to actively listen to the lecture because you still have to choose what to write down. However, it provides you with the details you need if there is a section of your notes that doesn't ring a bell when you are studying later. Another stylus-based software program is Penultimate, which allows you to use a stylus to take notes. Given a choice, you are still better off writing by hand than writing on a laptop, but these programs will allow you to use your tablet as a notebook. Another way to deal with notes is to take the notes in class, then transcribe them into your laptop or computer. If you are going to transcribe your notes or take notes during a lecture on a laptop (again, not a good strategy), it may be worth looking into some software that can help you organize and take notes. Software such as Evernote, Simplenote, and Microsoft OneNote are generally well reviewed for their ease of use and ability to help students organize their notes.

Important Points to Remember

Textbooks
✓ Prepare a productive study environment
✓ Textbooks work in conjunction with class lectures; knowing both makes success more probable

....

3 LOTS of research has been done on this recently, but this article in *The Atlantic* provides a great summary that outlines the most important points: http://www.theatlantic.com/technology/archive/2014/05/to-remember-a-lecture-better-take-notes-by-hand/361478/ (accessed October 10, 2015).

✓ Read course materials strategically—in small chunks, using outlines and notes, and *before* going to lecture
✓ Take notes strategically and by hand—don't use a laptop
✓ Studying a textbook or article is a process and it takes a bit of time; learning this process will save you time when you study for exams
✓ Supplemental texts and journal articles add detail and depth to the text and lectures

Taking Notes in Class
✓ Taking notes in class means understanding (not just memorizing) information about the topic for exams and other assessments
✓ Complete readings before class
✓ Review your notes from the previous class before the new lecture begins
✓ Do not write every word; writing less is more
✓ Handwrite your notes in class

Bibliography

Clump, M. A., Bauer, H., & Breadley, C. (2004). The extent to which psychology students read textbooks: A multiple class analysis of reading across the psychology curriculum. *Journal of Instructional Psychology, 31*(3), 227-32.

Willingham, D. T. (2002). Ask the cognitive scientist: Allocating student study time. *American Educator, 26*(2). http://dbweb01.aft.org/periodical/american-educator/summer-2002/ask-cognitive-scientist.

CHAPTER 3

ON THE MIDTERM GRIND

Students hate exams but what they don't know is that professors aren't huge fans of them either. Professors don't give exams because they enjoy grading (we don't) or even because they enjoy torturing students (although that is a perk!). We give exams to provide an incentive for students to really think about the material and because it is one of the few ways we can test whether students are doing the work and understanding the information sufficiently to pass the course. Ultimately, when the class is over, we have to provide a signal (via your letter grade) to you and others that you now know the material at some level and can move on to more advanced courses, or that you have sufficient knowledge to have your degree conferred.

So, as you approach each exam, you need to think about some important questions. First, what were you supposed to learn in this section of the course? More specifically, which concepts and theories should you understand, and what skills (e.g., critical thinking, analysis) should you have developed? Second, how does the professor expect you to illustrate that learning has occurred? In other words, what type of exam will it be, and how long will you have to finish it? Finally, and perhaps most importantly, how can you best prepare yourself to illustrate what you've learned?

While we will discuss the specific types of exams below, there are a few basics that you should start with before each exam, regardless of its format. Make sure you have been following the suggestions from Chapter 2! If you have been following those suggestions regarding reading and taking notes on the textbooks and articles, attending class and paying attention to lectures, participating in course discussions, and reviewing your materials on a regular basis, you have already done the heavy lifting in preparation for your exams. Now your entire focus can be on organizing and studying the material.

Doing well on an exam is all about understanding the information and—most importantly—illustrating that understanding. If you haven't done so already, you should begin by organizing your course material. Look at your syllabus for an outline of the topics covered and at your notes from lectures and from the textbooks. These things were not assigned randomly, so you should be able to look at all that material and see a general outline of topics, theories, concepts, and evidence, in that order. Begin by organizing all the information you have learned by *topic area*. How are those topics related to one another? Do they build on one another, are they organized as competing explanations for the same behavior, or something else? (Hint: If there is an essay on the exam, it will probably ask you to tie at least a couple of the broader topics together and explain how they are related.) Within each topic area, what are the most important *ideas or theories addressed in the readings and lectures*? How do they relate to the general topic area? Can you explain the *arguments* underlying those ideas/behaviors using the appropriate *concepts*? Finally, can you summarize the *evidence* supporting them?

Once you've organized your study materials in this way and thought about these questions, you will have found that there is some information that you remember readily and will not need to go over again, while there is other information that either seems only somewhat familiar or that you do not recall at all. At the very least, you have a general idea of what you need to know and where you should spend most of your study time. But, before we move on to the types of exams, let's talk about the elephant in the room: the study guide.

The Professor Gave You a Study Guide—Lucky You! Or Not ...

Ahhhh!! Students love study guides almost as much as they hate exams, but that's because they aren't thinking about them critically. There are pros and cons to receiving a study guide before an exam. The obvious "pro" is that the professor is providing you with a way to narrow the focus of your studying for the exam by identifying a relatively small number of concepts and topics. This "gift" leads students to think that if they just memorize everything in the study guide, they will do well on their test. However, this miscalculation is the basis of two important "cons."

While providing a study guide often (but not always) means that your professor is reducing the breadth of what will be covered, it usually means that they will expect more depth in your knowledge of the material. If you are going to be tested on only 5 of the 50 things discussed in class and you have 75 minutes to illustrate that knowledge, you better know a large amount about those subjects or ideas! That means much more analysis and critical thinking about the material. This expectation leads to the second problem, which is that memorization will often not be enough. In other words, students think "study guide" = "memorizing terms" while professors think "study guide" = "an in-depth comprehension of key concepts AND the ability to discuss those concepts in a sophisticated way." To put it directly, reading and memorizing material is not the same as *studying* material. This conflict of expectations rarely works well for either side, but it is the unaware student who pays the price by failing to prepare and, consequently, receiving a low grade.

Organizing the material provides you with a systematic way to approach a large sum of information. The question becomes: What do you do with it once it is organized? This gets us to that important distinction between memorization and understanding. In a pure sense, memorization gives us the ability to recall information. This process can be important, for instance, in learning new vocabulary in foreign language classes. So the process has a time and place, but your social science professors are going to be concerned with whether you can go beyond simply recalling information to applying that information, which helps demonstrate you understand the intricate nature of the subject. Thus, we make distinctions between simply memorizing material versus understanding that material. David Congos of the University of Central Florida has succinctly summarized the distinction between the two processes (see Table 3.1).

As you can see, understanding requires a fundamentally deeper understanding about subject matter than just memorizing key facts and ideas. While we can memorize facts about a subject (which helps during trivia night at the pub), an understanding of the material conveys the ability to make connections and to critically approach a subject (which helps during essay examinations that come before trivia night at the pub).

Study Groups

A study group can be a useful tool in preparing for an exam. In an ideal world, study groups are attractive because they provide a check on whether other students think of the material in the same way (i.e., how important is this term or idea?), and they divide the labor of studying among several people. They also allow each member to bring their strengths to the group so that everyone benefits. In a course on microeconomics, for example, one student might understand opportunity costs really well, while another is able to explain marginal costs and revenue with ease. You have the opportunity to help each other. Thus, there are tremendous benefits to study groups. So what are the drawbacks?

Many of the drawbacks to study groups deal with issues of self-discipline. Students who are not sharply focused on the material or prepared for the group

TABLE 3.1 Memorizing versus Understanding

MEMORIZING	UNDERSTANDING
Limits learning of ideas and concepts to word-for-word recall—this makes application of the concepts difficult	Converts ideas and concepts into own words—if you can put technical words and ideas into your own language, you have a better base for understanding it and explaining it to others
Limits ability to generate insight or creative ideas	Creates a basis for generating insights and creative syntheses
Limits learning to actual words recalled	Advances depth of learning
Inability to deduce or induce	Develops insights that come from deduction or induction
Has trouble seeing beyond the basic concept or idea	Can see meaning, effects, results, and consequences beyond the basic idea or concept
Difficult to explain ideas to someone else other than word-for-word	Able to use own words to explain something clearly to someone else
Difficult to see how ideas apply in the real world	Can apply ideas to real-world situations
Relevance of ideas outside the classroom is difficult to see	Promotes the ability to seek connections between knowledge learned in classroom and the outside world
Does not see differences, similarities, and implications of ideas	Can identify differences, similarities between ideas, and implications of these ideas
Interprets ideas literally	Realizes that there can be figurative as well as literal interpretations of ideas
Has trouble solving problems when numbers or components are changed	Can solve problems even when numbers or components are changed
Believes there is one right answer to every question	Accepts that there may be more than one "right" answer to a question depending on circumstances

Reproduced with permission, Dennis H. Congos, Learning Skills Specialist—Semi-retired, 120 Beech Street, Oviedo, FL 32765, dcongos@mail.ucf.edu

can be a distraction. The group may turn to idle gossip or complaining about other students or the professor. These distractions result in wasted time for you and the entire group. A few suggestions on working with study groups (which we also apply to group projects later) can help. First, make sure you and the other group members are dedicated to one purpose—studying. You should be free to tell the other group members that you are focused on this purpose and will depart if the group loses focus. You should be selfish with your study time! Second, construct a plan of responsibility that will be clear in terms of each person's responsibilities. If a person has not done their work (which we differentiate from not understanding the work, which is the purpose of the study group), then they probably should not be part of the group. Getting all the benefits of group work is unfair if you are not contributing (remember free-riders from Chapter 1?). Finally, make certain all members of the group are going to attend the meetings. If members do not make it to the meetings (with exceptions for problems and emergencies), then they should not have access to the work that the group will complete at that meeting. All these suggestions mean you need to have responsible, dedicated people for groups to work effectively—just like you would expect to see at your first job!

Types of Exams and Strategies for Each

Exams come in many forms, sometimes using more than one. They can be take-home or in-class, open or closed book, oral or written, multiple-choice, short answer, identification, or essay. Students have their clear favorites—usually because they are under the misapprehension that they can study less for some of them—but it is important to understand that preparation for each type should be the same, even while the process of taking the tests is different. Every time a professor offers a study guide or an "easier" type of exam (e.g., take-home), their expectations of what you will provide usually increases. So it is critical that you understand basic test taking strategies that apply to all types of examinations.

Basic Test Taking Strategies
✓ Read the whole exam before starting
✓ Know what each section of the exam is worth and allocate your time accordingly
✓ Use all the available class time to take the exam, but keep an eye on the clock

---

Read the whole exam before starting. Make sure you look at each section of the exam and read the instructions carefully. Don't lose points because you didn't realize there was something on the back of the last sheet that you missed or because you didn't follow simple instructions. If you don't understand what is being asked of you, ask the professor or proctor for clarification before you start. One professor we know wanted to emphasize the importance of following directions to his students. He started a multiple-choice exam with this instruction: "Read the entire examination first." On the last page, the exam said, "Now that you have read the entire examination, ignore all the questions, put your name on the answer sheet, and give it to your teaching assistant. You have an automatic 100% for this examination." Those that did not follow the instructions had their entire examination graded in the normal manner.

Know what each section of the exam is worth and allocate your time accordingly. The value that the professor assigns to each section is a signal to you of how much effort they expect you to put forward. If there are 25 multiple-choice questions and one essay and each of those two sections is worth 50 per cent of the exam grade, you should plan to spend 50 per cent of your time on each. In a 50-minute class, too many students may rush through the multiple-choice part in 10 minutes and spend 40 minutes on the essay. When this happens, students often lose easy points on the multiple-choice by not reading the questions carefully while providing more information than is needed on the essay. This strategy ultimately hurts your overall grade. Likewise, if your examination has identification sections that are worth 20 per cent of your exam and essays worth 80 per cent of your exam, you should tackle the essays first, even if the identification is listed first. Most likely, unless your professor makes a specific point of it, he or she is not going to care about the order in which you have answered the questions on the exam. The exception to this will be the order in which you answer your multiple-choice examination, particularly if you are using a Scantron sheet to mark your answers. In this case, you will want to be extra cautious about the order in which you answer all of your multiple-choice questions. We will talk about this issue a bit later.

Use all the available class time to take the exam, but keep an eye on the clock. There are three types of students—those who turn in the exam within 15 minutes of receiving it, those who take a large percentage of the class time but aren't rushed at the end, and those who don't allocate their time wisely, rushing through the last few questions. The first usually fail, the second tend to average significantly higher grades, while the third do well on the part of the exam they finish, but then lose points by not having time to carefully answer the final questions.

By studying strategically and following these three basic rules, you can perform your best on every exam. Now let's move on to the different exams themselves and strategies for approaching them.

Multiple Guess (Choice) Exams—Being Better than Chance

Students almost always say they prefer multiple-choice exams over any others, but then complain that the questions are tricky or confusing. However, every professor knows that students, on average, perform poorly on this type of test. There are likely many reasons for this disconnect, but the most important is this: students often equate multiple-choice examinations with pure memorization, usually of definitions for critical terms. Unfortunately for students, professors don't just focus multiple-choice questions on definitions. Multiple-choice questions can do so much more! For example, they can be designed to test whether students can connect or compare multiple concepts in an applied way. Those types of questions aren't "tricky," but they do require respondents to have a more dense understanding of the material. Simply being aware of the broad range of skills and knowledge that can be tested with multiple-choice questions is half the battle. The other half is preparation and studying to develop the skills and knowledge needed for these types of questions. Regardless of the topics and nature of the multiple-choice questions your professor may ask, there are specific multiple-choice strategies to keep in mind. At the least, you know that one of the answers is the correct one. Woohoo! But choosing which one…

Multiple-Choice Exam Strategies
- ✓ Always begin by reading the whole question carefully
- ✓ Read every answer just as carefully
- ✓ Strike through every obviously wrong answer
- ✓ Be wary of answers that include the words "never" and "always"
- ✓ If you narrow down your choices to two answers and simply cannot decide which is right, go with your gut feeling
- ✓ Record all your answers at the same time

Always begin by reading the whole question carefully. Too often, we read the words we expect to see rather than what is actually written on the page. In doing so, students will often see keywords and assume they know what the question is asking. Make a strong effort to read every word, and spend a minute making sure you understand what the question is asking. Students lose many points on questions they know the answer to largely because they failed to read the question correctly.

Read every answer just as carefully. Sometimes the options vary by a single word. Make sure you can see how each answer is different from the others.

Strike through every obviously wrong answer. Professors don't like writing multiple-choice questions. They're hard to make challenging but not tricky. It also means coming up with at least three wrong answers that could appear right to someone who doesn't understand the material. Sometimes we put in obviously wrong answers that should help in narrowing down the answer if you know the material. Try to identify those first.

Be wary of answers that include the words "never" and "always." Very few social scientists feel comfortable using those words because almost (see?) everything we study is conditional and deals more with patterns than definite conditions. We tend to qualify our explanations with words like "usually" and "under most conditions," so think twice if any absolute terms are used in an answer.

If you narrow down your choices to two answers and simply cannot decide which is right, go with your gut feeling. If you've truly studied for the exam in all the ways we have suggested, your instinct will be right more often than not. Circle your answer on the examination or write the letter or number of the choice in big letters next to the question.

Record all your answers at the same time. If your examination is *all* multiple choice and you are being asked to record your answers on a scan sheet or a Scantron, record your answers all at once in the last 10 minutes you have for the examination. This procedure seems counter-intuitive, but it is a way to avoid mistakes as you are rushing to answer the questions. If you are rushing from question to scan sheet back to questions, you can easily make a mistake in filling in the wrong number or the wrong answer to the question on your scan sheet. If you do them all at once toward the end of the examination, you can focus on just filling in the answers. This little hint is about avoiding the problems multitasking can create and avoiding small errors that can cost you big points. All it takes is for you to record your answers for one question in the wrong space on the scan sheet and everything that follows from that will also be wrong.

Identification and Short Answer

These exam questions can come in many different forms. Sometimes they require that you provide a simple definition for a term or a definition and an explanation of why the term is important. Other short answer questions ask you to briefly explain a theory or compare two concepts. The possibilities are endless, but your professor will probably prefer one type of short answer given the subject matter of the exam. So what are your strategies for this type of exam?

> **Strategies for Short Answer Questions**
> ✓ Find out what your professor means by "short answer"
> ✓ Provide a short but complete answer—definitions are not enough!

Find out what your professor means by "short answer." What type of information are they looking for? Do they just want definitions or should an example be included? Do they want you to explain why a term is important or relate it to another concept? It is important to understand their expectations, and maybe even ask if they can provide you with an example of a good answer before the exam. If you are in doubt, define the term, explain why it is important, and provide a brief example of it. Let's look at an example from economics where

the professor has provided the term "supply shock" in the short answer part
of her examination. The student may respond in this manner:

> Supply shock: a sudden or unexpected increase or decrease in the
> supply of a commodity that results in a change in the commodity's
> price. Shocks can be important in commodity pricing for consumers.
> If there is no change in consumption, a positive shock can decrease
> prices while a negative shock can increase prices. In 1997, an unexpected
> freeze damaged Brazil's coffee crops, causing a spike in global coffee
> costs, raising coffee prices for consumers as producers passed on the
> increased costs to consumers.

The answer contains three things: the definition, the possible effects and
importance of supply shocks, and an applied example using the Brazilian
coffee supply shock.

Provide a short but complete answer. Students can provide short answers that
aren't wrong, per se, but are not complete. For example, consider an exam
asking you to define and explain the political significance of the term "retrospective voting." A short, technically correct, but incomplete answer might be:

> When voters vote based on what has happened in the past. It's
> important because it is an explanation of why voters vote the way
> they do.

This answer is a bit frustrating for the student and professor. It is not wrong,
but it's not right either. More specifically, it's a statement of the obvious. Yes,
it's a way to explain why people vote in the manner they do. But the topic in
the syllabus is exactly about that subject, so it really doesn't explain why it's
important in the context of understanding why voters behave the way that
they do. As such, the significance is barely more than a restatement (in a more
general way) of the definition. A better way to answer this may be:

> Retrospective voting is the theory that voters will vote for the party in
> power if they are happy with the policy outcomes of the recent past and
> will vote for the challenging party if they are not. It is important because
> it suggests that voter choices are the result of incumbent behavior only
> and limits the impact of challenger behavior on election outcomes.

What is better about this answer? First, it notes that retrospective voting
is a *theory.* It gives a brief, but more *detailed explanation* of what that theory is,
and it provides a significance that *relates the term to some other concept*—the fact

that challengers have little control over their success—illustrating the ability to connect multiple discussions in the class.

Essays—The Demon Spawn Rears Its Ugly Head

Students often view essays as an evil presence. Much loathed and often misunderstood by students, essay questions are liked by many professors because they provide plenty of opportunity for students to demonstrate a deeper understanding of the material. The flipside of that statement is that essay questions also provide students with plenty of opportunity to bullshit. Yes, we used the term "bullshit," which has been the subject of several intellectual and academic treatises because it has become so prevalent in our discourse (see for instance Harry Frankfurt's 1986 *New York Times* bestseller *On Bullshit* and Andrew Aberdein's 2006 examination of Frankfurt's treatise in "Raising the Tone: Definition, Bullshit, and the Definition of Bullshit").

What is meant by bullshit? In general, essays that are layered with deep, thick bullshit occur when students are taken aback by the question and try to pass tangential and unrelated information as an answer. Keep in mind, your professors are generally considered experts in their field, so successfully doing this is quite difficult (though, in all fairness, professors are often referred to as professional bullshitters, so we say this with the idea that we are just better at it than you are). What constitutes an essay filled with lots of bullshit? Joking aside, there are four things that you want to avoid in writing your essays.

Four Things to Avoid in Essay Writing
✗ Vague definitions
✗ Providing examples instead of principles
✗ Large quotes from readings and lectures without explaining them or giving any context
✗ Writing on a related subject but not the subject about which the professor has asked

Vague definitions. From our previous examples, a clue may be "a supply shock is when there is a shock to the supply of a product"—the sentence is circular, indirect, and vague, indicating that the respondent does not know how to attack the definition head-on.

Providing examples instead of principles. For instance, suppose an anthropology professor asks a question about theories and concepts associated with primates and the evolution of primates. The student, not being prepared for the theory part of the question, decides to answer it with background and

stories from Jane Goodall's experiences with chimpanzees without addressing relevant theories. Is the information useful? Sure, and it could be part of
a good essay. Is it completely relevant? Only if it paired with the information that the professor is seeking in the answer. So, if you use Jane Goodall's
experiences as an example of her theories and concepts (or of others'), then
the essay begins to have more depth than if the respondent just talks about
Jane Goodall's funny, endearing, and even moving stories about chimpanzees.

*Large quotes from readings and lectures without explaining them or giving any
context.* Quotes are fine, but when they substitute for a direct explanation of
concepts, ideas, and theories, they are just essay filler. Your professor most likely
will like that you read, but what you do with the information matters more
than just regurgitating quotes without context or demonstrating a deeper
understanding.

Writing on a related subject but not the subject about which the professor has asked.
For instance, if a professor asks an essay question that deals with theories of
civil wars and the student responds with an essay focused on wars between
states, the student has responded to a similar topic, but not *the* topic the professor has posed.

This is not to say that what you may be doing is deceptive; these types of
answers tend to be natural defensive responses to do *something* in a moment
of panic, possibly as a result of not being prepared for or focused on the question. It can also be a response to not thinking and reacting to the question
systematically. You might get so excited about a topic in an essay that you just
start writing about the topic quickly; in doing so, you may forget to include
key parts that would make your essay better and more detailed.

Essay questions themselves can run the gamut from extremely short to
extremely long and descriptive questions in multiple parts. Shorter essay topics
(e.g., "Why war? Explain.") tend to be much more open, giving you freedom
to craft an answer specific to what you understand about the topic. Longer
essays with multiple parts are designed to direct you to a much narrower body
of knowledge your professor wants to see from you. Both types (and all those
in between) require you to provide a logical, well-organized, clearly written
answer, but how you get there may differ with the style of the question, which
means there are costs and benefits to each type of question.

Benefits of less prescriptive (short) essay questions. These questions allow students
to format the answer in a way they feel most comfortable and give them the
opportunity to focus on the concepts and theories they are most comfortable discussing.

Costs of less prescriptive (short) essay questions. Unfortunately, the lack of guidance on these questions means that it is easy for students to go (far) off topic.
Answers can be unstructured and rambling. Even if the professor gives you the

opportunity to structure the essay in a manner that you prefer, you still need to use the opportunity to illustrate specific material that you learned in the course. If the professor asks the "Why war?" question noted above, it is probably because he or she has provided you with a variety of theories about why nations go to war. Your answer should be structured around comparing those theories and talking about the strengths and weaknesses of each of them. In the course of generating this answer, be sure to correctly use related concepts and ideas. Students writing essay exams are rarely rewarded by just listing various theories or concepts, so be sure to explain them in the course of your essay. Remember, you are trying to illustrate the breadth and depth of your newly gained knowledge; if you simply regurgitate terms learned in the class, it makes the professor think you've memorized the names of the terms but may not understand what they mean or how they relate to the topic at hand.

Benefits of long, detailed essay questions. Some instructors are control freaks (including one of the authors of this book … we'll let you guess which one), and there is specific information they want covered in their essay questions. These professors tend to write essay questions that are longer and provide students with more direction to how the answers should be structured.

Costs of long, detailed essay questions. They are really asking for specific information that you need to know. This type of question means you have less leeway in terms of what you may choose to include; the professor wants specific information from you.

No matter the nature of the question, a few strategies can be useful in tackling these questions, particularly if you are faced with a time crunch (which will be a frequent occurrence in your academic career).

Strategies for Essay Questions
✓ Be organized about the answer: start with an outline
✓ Always include an introduction and conclusion
✓ In the body of your essay, explain your argument
✓ If you are running out of time, outline the rest of your answer

Be organized about the answer. No matter how long the question is and how long your answer is going to be, *outline* your answer first before you start writing. This process will serve two purposes. First, it will keep your answer organized so that you are not just writing off the top of your head. Unstructured essays tend to ramble and not get to the point. Second, it will ensure that you cover the necessary points needed to answer all parts of long questions. In complex questions, the professor is asking for specific information. If you are writing off the top of your head, it is easy to miss a key part of the question. Why chance that when you are rushing to write the essay? The outline does not have to be long and detailed, just a quick jotting of points to be covered in the essay to remind you to do so. What should you include in your outline? The answer to this question depends on the type of question that your professor is asking. You want to sketch out some main ideas that will take the reader through your answer. A basic outline to a straightforward question that asks you to use an approach or theory or to compare them in an essay should include an introduction and conclusion, an explanation of your argument, and the theories and principles you are using as support.

Always include an introduction and conclusion. You want to outline a few bullet points that offer some background and the answer to your question. The introduction should provide (a) a brief background statement on the topic, (b) the answer(s) that you are going to support (i.e., what is your thesis or what is the argument you are going to put forward to answer the question?), and (c) how you will support it (theories and examples you will use). Your introduction should be a direct hit at the answer to the question—no beating around the bush. For instance, if you are asked to compare two theories, tell the reader in the introduction, "Based on the evidence, theory X is more useful than theory Y in explaining the issue." The conclusion should reiterate all this information and highlight the important points you have made in answering your question. It should tell the reader the lesson to take away from the answer and how your evidence and examples support that lesson.

In the body of your essay, explain your argument. You want to include the key theories or ideas you will draw upon to help you arrive at your answer, being sure to define key concepts and explain core principles. For your outline, create bullet points for the key principles you need to include. Make sure that you include appropriately defined concepts if they are needed to understand your approach. As part of the body to the essay, you may also highlight examples of what you are discussing in the section on key theories. Provide a small bit of background with your examples and explain how your key theories or principles apply to the case. (Don't leave it to your professor to make the connections; we already know them. We want to make sure you understand the links!)

Now that you have spent a minute or two outlining the answer, look at it carefully. Does it have a flow or logic that makes sense? Are you missing a key concept or idea? Are you able to define those concepts clearly? Most importantly, does it actually answer the question?

If you are running out of time, outline the rest of your answer. If you are up against the clock, take the last minute or two to at least outline the answer you wanted to give so your professor knows where you were heading and that you had the ideas and examples to finish—you were just up against time.

Some professors will appreciate this and not think that you just dropped the ball. You may get some credit, and some credit is better than no credit. It's not the perfect answer you may have envisioned, but it will provide your professor with a sense of how you were going to move forward with the essay. A conclusion should discuss your major points and what the reader should have learned from the essay. Does the essay show the strengths and weaknesses of a theory or a problem with a case? What are they? Does the essay question ask you to compare theories or cases? Which is stronger and why?

Now that your examination is over, the only thing to do is to wait for the results and to evaluate what went right and what went wrong.

Getting Your Grade

Grades are often the most stressful part of being at college or university. Most students get them, though there are a few colleges and universities that do not issue grades, instead providing evaluation reports about the student's performance. Grades are necessary, but many professors do not like having to issue them. Sometimes we want to emphasize the positive elements of educating our students, and grades are stark—there is little gradation or nuance. When we issue a grade, we do not get a chance to say here is what is good and here is what needs improvement. There is not much explanation unless the professor takes time to issue long feedback on assignments. So without the nuance, students are left to wonder what grades mean. Remember that your grades say nothing about who you are as a person. *You are not a better or worse person because of a grade.* While a low grade may be disappointing and a high grade may justify your approach to the exam (and even boost your ego a bit), try not to personalize your grades. Your grade is reflective of your performance at that time under that professor. If these factors change, your grades may change accordingly.

You need to be realistic about what to expect from your grades. If you are carrying six courses, working part-time, and volunteering at a non-profit organization while trying to have a social life, you may find that something has to give way. Most often, it is going to be your class performance. Balancing your true time demands and your expected final grade outcome has to be a realistic endeavor. It may also be the case that you learn better with professors who have an approach that, for example, is more visual or uses different types of assignments. While we generally say that your grade is what you have earned (and this is indeed true), it is also the case that many factors go into your final grade and the outcome could be different at another time or under another professor.

Taking Charge of Your Education

It has also been our experience that sometimes a student's grades are a sign of other things that may not be going well in the student's life. As we have said before, college or university is a big change, and the pressures you feel can be significant at times. You may feel overwhelmed or even just homesick if you are far away from home for the first time. If you are experiencing personal problems that are interfering with your class performance, you should talk to your professor or someone at your college or university. Colleges and universities usually have student support services available for those who are experiencing personal problems and issues (such as a death in the family) or mental health issues. If you are unsure where to find these, check your institution's orientation material or websites. If you are still having trouble, you should feel free to speak to your academic advisor or even to your professor, who can point you to the appropriate student support services. Discussing your problems with college personnel such as counselors or advisors is important because they can communicate with your professors and make them aware that you are experiencing problems that need attention or consideration (usually without breaking confidentiality if you are concerned with such issues). Your professors can sometimes lend a friendly ear, but keep in mind that most of them are not professional counselors and, if you are in crisis, they will need to help you find a trained professional.

Nonetheless, after you consider everything regarding your grade, you may find that you are unhappy with your performance in the class. You need to assess what happened during the semester and not get discouraged. You need to be proactive when it comes to rectifying problems that you may be having. It is worthwhile to start this process at the beginning of the semester.

Keep your own grading records. Either in a spreadsheet or with your notes, keep track of the class, the assignment, your grade, what it is worth, and a running total that shows your current grade. Analyze your grades every time you get an assignment back. In some cases, you may find that you only have two grades (a midterm and final examination); in other cases, you may find you have lots of grades to track (weekly quizzes, projects, examinations … all in the same class).

Reevaluate your strategy. If you find a trend, such as doing poorly in routine quizzes, it may be time to reevaluate your strategy and talk to your professor, teaching assistants, and academic support teams. Do not get stuck with only one method of doing things if that method is failing. Just because one strategy works in your anthropology class does not mean it is going to work in your economics class. Be flexible and willing to adopt new approaches; the worst thing you can do is nothing—be proactive about changing up things when they are not working in a particular class.

Seek help and input at the first sign of trouble. The sooner you can discuss problems with those who can assist you, the more options will be available to help you. Almost every semester, we have students who come to us at the last moment (usually final exam period) to ask us what they can do to improve their grades. But by that time, everything is riding on that one exam, or worse, the final exam can't even help them! Be aware of your grades early and allow your professors and other staff to help you before this becomes so critical you are in danger of doing poorly. Remember, doing poorly on one quiz might be easily explained, but three in a row might be a problem that needs to be discussed.

Evaluate all your classes. At the end of the term, if you did well in all of your classes, that is wonderful and you should take pride in that! If not, look at your grades and see what went wrong in each class. At that point, you need to develop a plan to make sure this pattern does not repeat the next semester. Grades are not everything, but for those who want to have a solid record moving into an advanced degree or need good grades for post-graduation jobs, *you should be active in managing your grades* and evaluating the results of your efforts. Achieving strength and knowledge in your subject area is a process of constantly improving. If you do find problems in your performance, it may not be a bad idea to discuss your final grade with the professor or teaching assistant who can provide some insight into the critical issues that led to your grade.

But what if you think you have done everything correctly? What if you think that there is a problem with your grade and that it lies with those who did the evaluation (your professor or teaching assistant)? In some cases, the grade may be the result of a small miscalculation and the issue can be fixed quite easily. Most professors are good about this and will easily fix grades that result from miscalculations. What if you think the grade is a result of a different interpretation of the material, or even an oversight in the material on the part of the professor or teaching assistant? This type of concern is something that you want to handle professionally and wisely. There are a few steps that you can take, and probably should take, in thinking about challenging grades during or after the semester. Grade issues are a common concern for students. They are such a concern that we wrote these tips as part of a Wikihow entry.[1] These tips are based on balancing grade concerns from both the student's and the professor's perspective.

Before starting a grade appeal, determine if you have a legitimate basis to ask your professor for a grade review. From your standpoint, you may not understand how or why you got the grade that you did. But you also need to understand the side you may not often see—how and why professors grade in the manner in which they do. Professors must treat everybody fairly and equitably when it comes to grading. When professors grade papers or exams, they try their best to apply the same standards to every paper. For instance,

1 Wikihow, "How to Get a Professor to Change Your Grade," http://www.wikihow.com/Get-a-Professor-to-Change-Your-Grade.

when we grade papers, we don't necessarily want to see the student's name. We flip the cover pages over on all the papers and just read. That helps us to block out any name bias we may have. If a professor reads an exam or paper again, that very act is giving that paper or exam extra consideration which others in the class will not have. Therefore you must have a legitimate academic reason for the professor to give you extra consideration. You might be unhappy with your grade, but you need to determine honestly how your grade got to that state before you can challenge it.

How to Question or Appeal a Grade
- ✓ Make sure you have read and followed the instructions in the syllabus and on the assignment correctly and that you have read your professor's comments in their entirety
- ✓ Think about the overall context of the grade when you receive it
- ✓ If you challenge your grade, always conduct yourself in a professional manner
- ✓ Make an appointment with the professor or graduate assistant
- ✓ If a teaching assistant did the grading, address your questions/ problems with them first
- ✓ Prepare for the meeting
- ✓ Be courteous and professional in the meeting with the assistant or professor
- ✓ Highlight specific areas of concern and ask for an explanation of went wrong in those areas
- ✓ Take it to a higher level as a last resort

Make sure that you have read and followed the instructions in the syllabus and on the assignment correctly and that you have read your professor's comments in their entirety. Also make sure that you have followed instructions in their entirety. Often, confusion over grades comes from a lack of understanding about the reason for a grade.

Think about the overall context of the grade when you receive it. If you are challenging 2 points on a quiz that is worth 100 points and the quiz is only worth 5 per cent of your final grade, is it really worth it to go through this hassle? Before you make a decision about challenging a grade, think about the bigger picture: How much can you really gain in the final analysis? If the answer is potentially a substantial amount, then you should move forward, because that type of mistake or issue can have a large impact on the final grade you receive.

If you challenge your grade, always conduct yourself in a professional manner. Professors try to evaluate students' work based on performance and results.

When you get to college, you may find that what used to get you straight A's in high school may not be enough to get you that grade in college. You may need to retool your approach, and there are people certainly willing to help with that. But you want to avoid unprofessional behavior such as temper tantrums (in person or via email), threatening to tell the professor's "superiors," or suing the professor or the college or university.

Make an appointment with the professor or graduate assistant. Talk to your professor or assistant and learn how you might improve the quality of your work on the next assignments. Professors look favorably upon students who put a concerted effort into learning the material and do their best to improve their knowledge and skills, as opposed to merely focusing on the grade. Try not to appeal a grade during class, when the professor has a room full of students to teach. Instead, go to office hours or set up an appointment. Professors notice thoughtful, respectful behavior.

If a teaching assistant did the grading, address your questions/problems with them first. Ask to make an appointment with the teaching assistant to discuss the matter. Bypassing the teaching assistant may make the assistant feel slighted. Likewise, most professors who have teaching assistants should tell you to discuss the matter with the assistant first.

Prepare for the meeting. Read all the feedback you received. If the instructor has taken points off that you thought you deserved, go back into your lecture notes and text books and make a list of supporting evidence to take to the meeting. Be able to show the professor that you had the correct information, that you knew the material well, and that you were prepared. Use the evidence as a basis for asking the professor or assistant to reconcile it with what he or she wanted in the paper or exam.

Be courteous and professional in the meeting with the assistant or professor. Do not be accusatory—avoid phrases like "I don't think that you like me," or "I think I'm being treated unfairly." Professors can only evaluate the work in front of them. They cannot give you a grade you did not earn just because they like you. Avoid telling the professor "I did the same thing my friends did in the class and got a lower grade." Their grades are not relevant to the discussion, and confidentiality rules will prevent a professor from discussing other students' grades. Further, a student learning a new topic for the first time does not have the insight to accurately gauge if two answers are "the same thing." While two answers might seem identical to you, each student's work has differences in content and delivery that convey to a professor whether each student "gets it" or "doesn't get it."

Highlight specific areas of concern and ask for an explanation of what went wrong in those areas. Your professor or assistant should be able to demonstrate clearly where you went wrong. If the answer is not consistent with lecture notes or the textbook from which you got your information, then ask for clarification:

"Professor X, I think I understand what you have said, but I'm a bit confused because I thought from your lecture on (whatever subject or date) you said _____" or "I think I understand what you've said, but in the textbook, it seems to be saying something different and this is how I understood it." If the professor is clearly in the wrong and a mistake was made, most often the professor will concede. If the professor makes her or his point and it is consistent with all the information you have written, point out to the professor the consistency between the lectures, books, and the information you just received in the discussion. Let the professor try to elaborate on any information that you may be missing, or let her or him justify the grade in light of that information. If you show that there is strong consistency between your learning materials (lectures and notes) and what you wrote, the professor will usually reconsider the point deduction or even the grade itself.

Take it to a higher level as a last resort. If all else fails, most academic departments have processes in place to appeal grades to committees. This process usually starts with the undergraduate director or chair of the department. Keep in mind that it is extremely rare for professors to overturn another professor's grade unless there is a clear and compelling reason to do so. However, if there clearly is a miscarriage of justice, a good compromise can often be worked out, or a committee hearing can be scheduled to review the grade complaint. Make sure you can document that you have been wronged and that there is evidence for it. The best outcome is that the situation is resolved amicably and all parties are happy; the worst is that you will have spent time and energy on a futile exercise and damaged your own reputation in the process. Again, weigh the costs against the benefits and decide if this is something worth doing.

Within all of this, a few caveats are probably in order. Some professors will ask you to write out your reasons for challenging the grade. Professors do this so that you organize and focus your thoughts, and to give you time to get past any initial emotional reactions. The issue is then in front of them and can be judged on its merits. This procedure can discourage students from challenging their grade without good reason, and it gives students who have valid challenges the opportunity to present their cases clearly. Some professors may also have a policy that if they review your test or paper, the entire exam or paper is up for reevaluation. This can have its positives and negatives. The positives are obvious, but the negatives can outweigh the positives; a professor can then find other things wrong with the paper or exam and use it as a basis to lower your grade further.

Also understand that each discipline has its own way of doing things. Writing an anthropology paper is different than writing a paper for economics or sociology. Avoid approaching your professor and telling her or him that it's done another way in some other discipline; it is your responsibility to adapt to the requirements of this professor and the discipline. It is also the case that many colleges and universities forbid the changing of final grades, except in cases of "computational error." The reason for this prohibition is that disputes over grades can consume enormous amounts of time for students and faculty. Generally, no one can change the grade a professor gives—not the chair or department head, not the dean or president—though procedures vary from college to college and department to department.

Do not make the mistake of assuming that professors and instructors always grade unemotionally. However, instances of obvious bias (intentionally or not) are rare. Also, instructors who consistently grade based on emotion will eventually be discovered by students. One complaint above the professor's head will not have much influence, since most chairs assume that professors have good evaluative judgment; however, a pattern of complaints will usually develop around a problematic faculty member.

Important Points to Remember

How to Succeed on Exams
- ✓ Don't overestimate the value of a study guide
- ✓ Know the details of the exam ahead of time—e.g., type of exam and time allowed—and strategize your test taking accordingly
- ✓ Use all the time available to take the exam and allocate that time wisely
- ✓ Make sure you fully understand your professor's expectations

Getting Your Grade
- ✓ Keep your own grading records
- ✓ Reassess your study and exam strategies on a regular basis
- ✓ Ask for personal or academic help earlier rather than later
- ✓ When asking questions about or challenging a grade, be organized, prepared, professional, and respectful

---

Bibliography

Aberdein, A. (2006). *Raising the tone: Definition, bullshit, and the definition of bullshit.* Chicago: Open Court.

Frankfurt, H.G. (1986). *On bullshit.* Princeton, NJ: Princeton University Press.

CHAPTER 4

FINDING YOUR CURIOSITY AND RESEARCH ZEN: SKILLS AND THE PROJECTS THAT BUILD THEM

The nature of the modern workforce has put a premium on skills that you may not think about while you are in school. In fact, students often avoid professors who assign "large" or "difficult" projects that could help them develop these skills. Part of contemplating why you are at a college or university is thinking about the type of skills you want to acquire to make you appealing to an employer and stand out from every other applicant applying for a position. As professors, we hope you are in school "for the love of education" or "to better the world" or "to make a difference." It's great if that is the case, and we love to see students who have this drive. But not all students want to become academics, nor do we expect that of you. Most professors also know that the large majority of students are looking to garner the experience they need to start their career or even land their dream job. That means that part of our job as professors is to help prepare you for life after college and to impart skills that will be useful once you leave our classrooms. It may not always be apparent, but many (if not most) of your professors have worked non-academic jobs and can provide insight into the types of skills that may prove useful outside of the university setting. The question that should be on your mind is "What skills do I need?"

This question is not easy to answer because every person's educational objectives are different. In 2012, the National Association of Colleges and Employers (NACE) completed a survey of hiring managers that asked them what skills they sought in new hires just coming out of colleges and universities. The top 10 answers are shown in the box (we have included the larger skills being emphasized in parentheses).

Skills Employers Are Seeking in New College/University Student Hiring

✓ Ability to work in a team (collaborative skills)
✓ Ability to make decisions and to solve problems (problem-solving skills)
✓ Ability to plan, to organize, and to prioritize work (organizational and analytical skills)
✓ Ability to communicate verbally with people inside and outside an organization (communication skills)
✓ Ability to obtain and to process information (research and analytical skills)
✓ Ability to analyze quantitative data (math and statistics—for social scientists, statistics are the key here)
✓ Technical knowledge related to the job (field-specific technical skills)
✓ Proficiency with computer software programs (computer skills)
✓ Ability to create and/or to edit written reports (writing skills—texting does not count here!)
✓ Ability to sell and to influence others (communication skills)

Source: National Association of Colleges and Employers, 2012

The extraordinary thing about this list is that these skills are not much different from what employers sought 30 years ago. The methods certainly have changed—for instance, PowerPoint, Prezi, and Impress now dominate how information is conveyed in oral presentations—but the need for communication skills has not. To varying degrees, you can acquire most of these skills as a social sciences major. It is up to you how refined and honed your skills will be when you leave your college or university.

When professors assign class projects, they are either implicitly or explicitly trying to impart to you a set of skills that are broad—research, communication, writing skills—or discipline-specific. Professors generally construct class projects with several objectives in mind. In the social sciences, the primary objectives usually involve giving students an opportunity either to apply what you have learned in the class or to acquire additional information related to the subject. In a class on legislative processes, for example, your professor may engage you in a parliamentary or congressional simulation; in an economics course, your professor may use a simulation to demonstrate "The Tragedy of the Commons." The objective in these assignments is to convey to you the complexity of these decision-making processes and to deepen your analytical skills. However, a professor in a course on international trade may have you do research on the tariff policies of a country. Such an assignment would allow you to expand your knowledge about a particular country while providing you insight into how countries approach trade policy. Both of these types of projects have components designed to enhance and practice research, communication, writing, and analytical skills. Being fully engaged and committed to these types of projects will provide you with opportunities to improve your skills—opportunities you may not get in other classes. With that being said, let's take a look at the kind of projects that you may encounter in your college or university career.

Finding Your Curiosity and Research Zen

Let's face it. You are going to be taking some classes that you have little interest in, at least initially. No matter how many pots of coffee you drink in the morning to make that 8 AM class, it will never be enough to make up for your lack of enthusiasm for the topic. But this is where you have to put the best face on the situation. Each class that you take is an opportunity to expand your intellectual horizons. A well-rounded person intellectually understands a bit about the world outside their bubble of interest. Why? Who cares if you know the formula for the force of gravity? Or the molecules that make up water? It's not just about personal growth, though this is important. It is also about making connections in the world (and doing well in pub trivia contests).

Colleges and universities are notorious for erecting disciplinary boundaries that often convey the idea that our world is neatly compartmentalized. Nothing could be farther from the truth, especially in the social sciences. It is not difficult to see that anthropologists and sociologists study groups and people affected by economics and political structures, or that economic behavior and political institutions are influenced by traditional belief systems around the world. Human behavior and interactions are complex and involve many areas of research. We can no longer say that we have an understanding of an issue because we have taken courses in economics or anthropology. Instead, our world is interdisciplinary, and understanding it requires the insight and skills of many approaches. All the social sciences can bring something to the table that gives us a better understanding of why social phenomena occur. Sometimes taking classes "outside your major" offers insights and ideas that provide you with a completely new worldview.

Let's give you an example of this process. For a long time, patents and patent laws had been considered an arcane, boring area of legal inquiry and practice. But at the end of the 1980s, this area became much more important as the knowledge economy blossomed around the world. This was also the period of the onset of the HIV/AIDS pandemic. What do they have to do with each other? Patents control access to medicines produced by pharmaceutical firms. They give firms the exclusive right to produce those medicines, meaning, in some countries, they can charge any price for the medicines. By itself, the field of patents is a technical legal area, but when you look at the social, economic, and political impact of patents, the research becomes a bit more complex. Patents may mean that developing countries affected by the HIV/AIDS pandemic do not receive or cannot afford necessary medicines. This problem raises issues that are connected to trade problems (trading in patent protected and enforced commodities), problems of morality and justice (how can only a few people have access to life-saving medicine?), political interests (how can the pharmaceutical industry affect a country's laws to improve their patent protections and what will be the social cost of it?), and even indigenous property issues (how have indigenous people had their traditional medicines stolen and sold for profit by pharmaceutical firms and research universities?). In a larger context, patents became a field of inquiry into the issue of inequality between states and control over who owns research, particularly when that research is supposed to save lives. What started as a boring, arcane legal field is now at the center of global debates about economics, anthropology, political science, and philosophy. All these fields have contributed to understanding the social phenomena around patents and patent protection.

What this means is that exposing yourself to a variety of classes can help you find your *curiosity Zen*. What interests you, and how can that interest be furthered through interaction with peers and professors who are accomplished in the area? What kind of topics drive you and make you want to know more? These are not just ideas to get the paper or project done. These are topics and ideas that tap into an inner core or spirit. For each course you take, you need to find what captures your attention. There is one basic reason for this: if you have a deep interest in a topic, it will make a class project much easier for you.

If you are developing a project for a class, the best thing that you can do is to *talk to your professor*! Your professor can discuss the details of the project while providing insights that you may have overlooked on your own. Finding your *curiosity Zen* is not a journey you take alone—the more people you talk to, the better the journey will be. With that in mind, you will encounter several different types of projects in your college career; professors design each of them to build a base of knowledge and skills.

Class Projects: Their Purposes and Some Helpful Suggestions

Research Projects

Research projects have been the core tool that professors have used to challenge their students because they require students to delve deeper into a specific topic within the context of the class. These are meant to be manageable topics that can be written within a semester (although final or honors theses are written over more than one semester). Professors differ in what they expect from a research paper, but often the professor is looking for more depth on a narrow topic than breadth on a general one. For instance, a paper on "How Russia Won World War II" may be a bit too broad in its scope, given that entire books have been written on this topic. But something more focused, like "Russian Military Strategy at the Battle of Stalingrad," might be more manageable for a semester research project. Similarly, a paper on "Islam's Impact on African History" might be a bit ambitious (just a tad!), but narrowing it down for an anthropology paper titled "Islam's Role in the Belief System of the Hausa People of Nigeria" is more manageable. Some professors will assign you a specific topic; in these cases you need to put the best spin on the situation and approach it with the idea that the professor is looking for something specific and has a reason for assigning the topic. Talk with your professor or teaching assistant about the boundaries and parameters for such papers. Is there some leeway in terms of how you approach the topic? Most professors have a range of ideas for research topics, so try to explore them with your professor.

Research papers serve several learning-related functions. Certainly, professors want you to obtain a greater understanding of the topic(s) they are reviewing in the class. But to do that, they also have to help build the relevant skills so you can get that deeper knowledge. Research papers thus become exercises in how to gather information, analyze that information in a logical way, construct and deconstruct arguments, and present valid, empirically supported conclusions. The depth of your knowledge becomes dependent upon how far you take your research. In thinking about this, you want to keep in mind that social science research is based on trying to understand why some social phenomena occur, not just describing the phenomena.

For example, since the end of World War II, scientists from across disciplines have been interested in the prevention of war, with researchers in the field of international relations taking the lead. Since that period, a host of interdisciplinary theories have emerged. Researchers in the area of political science, economics, philosophy, biology, psychology, sociology, statistics, mathematics, and anthropology have all made significant contributions to understanding the onset and duration of wars (Dougherty & Pfaltzgraff, 2001). Why something, such as war, occurs can be a complex question that takes you into many fascinating areas for research. Once again, discussions with your professor can help you to narrow your focus.

Summaries, Critiques, and Literature Reviews

These three types of projects have one thing in common: they are all based on past research on a topic. Summaries require you to provide a synopsis of a research paper, book, documentary, movie, or other type of work. In doing so, you may be answering these questions: What is the main argument the author is trying to address? How does the author build that argument? What evidence do they provide? What methodology do they use (i.e., how do they conduct their study—a particular case, a statistical model, reasoning, or logic)? The idea is not to stray too far from the basic elements of the original text. You want to present a condensed version of the author's important or essential ideas. Again, each professor will differ in how they want summaries to be presented, but generally a good summary can be written in one to two pages (double-spaced, of course).

Critiques follow the initial logic of summaries in that you are providing the reader with a summary of the essential information of the work you are examining. The goal of the critique differs in that you also want to provide your evaluation of that work. Critiques, however, are not just your opinion. You may not like the conclusion that the researcher or author reaches, but that is not enough for a critique. Critiques present both the positive and negative aspects of the work. Such an evaluation should be supported by both logic and reasoning or by other evidence you can provide. An example might help to illustrate this principle.

After summarizing an article where the author argues that states should intervene in other states to protect human rights, a student makes the following critique:

> I feel the author is wrong because we just can't be the world's police.

Such a statement is an *opinion*, and it really does not address anything that the author may have said. Consider this revised statement:

> While the author's argument has merit, the author has failed to take
> into account arguments and examples that may show this position's
> weaknesses. For instance, the author discusses the successes of US
> intervention in Somalia to protect the starving population; however, the
> author does not mention that multiple military personnel died in the

intervention. Thus, the author does not take into account the problems that can occur in human rights interventions.

This type of answer requires a bit more information, but it will be one that will get you more credit.

By looking at the author's argument closely, the student can present an informed evaluation instead of just an opinion. This element is key in analytical writing. Every student in your class can and will have opinions. But opinions are not persuasive if they simply sit by themselves. Critiques provide evidence of the strengths and weaknesses of arguments and ideas.

Finally, literature reviews are the most complex of the three writing assignments being discussed in this section. Most likely you did not have to do literature reviews during your high school career. Literature reviews can stand by themselves or they can be incorporated into a larger research project. The central question that literature reviews ask is "Why does my research need to be done?" In answering that question, you need to explain to your reader what research has already been done and why that research is insufficient at this point in time.

The literature review is an exercise in *critical assessment*. In completing the literature review, your goal is to analyze previous research on your topic to determine how valid or solid that research is. Are there biases in that research? Is it flawed in some way? Are there design or methodological problems (how the researcher conducted the study) in the research? Are there areas that researchers still need to explore? The literature review is not just listing a bunch of studies; *it tells a story* about the state of the research on a topic and presents a critical assessment, often so that you can highlight why more research may be needed on the topic. If your literature review is part of a larger research paper your professor assigns, then this is your opportunity to justify the approach you are taking in your research by highlighting deficiencies or needed areas of research on your topic. If the literature review will stand alone, then this is your opportunity to show why more research on a topic is needed. One of the best descriptions for writing literature reviews has been produced by the University of North Carolina at Chapel Hill's Writing Center, and we've listed the link to the description in the Web Links section at the end of the chapter.

Group Projects
In the vast range of words that exist in the English language, no two words strike more dread and fear into college students than when a professor stands in front of the class on Day 1 and utters these two words: "Group Project." At that point, social media begins to have a massive overload as students hyperventilate, posting and tweeting "OMG, this professor just assigned a *Group*

Project." This message is then usually followed by a string of words that suggest things the professor should do that are physically impossible. This is not an exaggeration. Here are a few of our favorite tweets about group projects and how students feel about them:

@jcblmbrt: "Twas the week before finals and all through the union, people in group projects were meeting and they all look like they hate each other."

@AngeeCrawford: "The Fact that I'm in 3 different group projects make me want to rip my hair out."

@AKcrazy18: "Group projects make me understand, why superman works alone."

@hwright24: "Can the next Iphone update make a 3 way FaceTime mode to help stressed students around the world with group projects!"

@JordanVictoriaa: "if there is a hell, im 100% positive that all they do there is group projects"

@sistachristaa: "when will professors realize that all we learn through group projects is hatred and distrust"

@dumbdolans: "group projects suck ass because I always end up doing the work"

@ashyy: "Which one of the presidential candidates doesn't support group projects in school?"

We have all had this feeling. It emanates from two real issues: part of your grade is not in your control and the final product is dependent upon people you may or may not know, or who may or may not have your work ethic (which is hopefully sound and responsible). Group projects can be more work for students and professors if done correctly; so why do professors assign them if they are so unpopular with students?

There is probably no assignment that better simulates what you will face in your real world career. In today's workplace, a single individual completes few, if any, jobs by herself or himself; you are always working within or between groups of people to finish projects of many kinds. This situation becomes more true as individual-level specialization increases and social and communications media flourish, allowing people to do projects from anywhere in the world. As noted earlier, one of the primary skills that employers seek is the ability to work in collaborative environments where everyone contributes. They value this because when multiple people participate in a project, alternative approaches and perspectives are revealed that an individual would not be able to devise on their own. This means that you need to learn to produce work with multiple individuals with different skills and expertise.

With that being said, we also know that group projects are filled with pitfalls and problems—most of which you will also find in the real world. These include conflicting schedules; irresponsible, lazy, or incompetent students/ co-workers; juggling multiple projects; and others taking credit for work they haven't done. The big difference between having these problems at a job and having these problems in class is that underperformers at work can be fired or dismissed from employment. Professors cannot do that in a classroom, but that does not mean they cannot exercise some control over the behavior of students within groups.

Professors have two ways to do this. First, they can allow students to rate each other's performance across a range of performance indicators specific to the group project. This rating can be a factor in each student's grade along with the grade for the group project. The professor can also allow the group to "fire" underperforming students by unanimous consent of all group members. This would be a clear indicator of the student's inability to work in a collaborative environment, a key component in any group project. The professor decides what to do with that information or what punishment to invoke. If these issues do concern you, discuss them with the class and professor to get a sense of how your professor might handle these types of issues. Meanwhile, we can offer some advice for dealing with group projects.

Making Group Projects Less Painful

Working Through Group Projects
- ✓ Meet early and frequently
  - Determine who is going to lead the project
  - Set initial deadlines for further meetings and for preliminary work to be done
  - Decide on logistics
  - Plan and brainstorm ideas
- ✓ Think about how your group will communicate
- ✓ Collectively review work
- ✓ Stay upbeat and positive as much as you can
- ✓ Communicate with the professor or assistant

Meet early and frequently. It is important to make sure you are able to meet to organize the project; meeting once is not enough. You need to get together frequently to make sure that everyone is on the same schedule and that everyone is doing what he or she is supposed to do. Your first meeting should have a few objectives:

- *Determine who is going to lead the project.* All projects should have someone that takes the lead in organizing and keeping everyone on track. Without leadership, most projects fail dismally. Do not be shy about stepping up and volunteering to organize things. Be careful, though, to emphasize that you are willing to organize aspects of the project but not do all of them by yourself! You will want to assign roles to other people: will someone act as editor of the work being done? Do you need someone to record the information from your meetings so that everyone understands what happened in the meeting? When it comes time to dividing work, the leader of the group can play an important role in understanding everyone's situation. If a member of the group has three group projects, an internship, and a part-time job, does it make sense to give her the most important part of the group project? A good leader will understand the group's collective and individual dynamics so that when it comes time to assigning work, problems can be intercepted before they affect the group's final product.

- *Set initial deadlines for further meetings and for preliminary work to be done.* The objective here is to make sure that work is getting done ahead of the deadlines set by your professor. Let technology be your friend in terms of staying organized and meeting deadlines. Mark your electronic calendars with key dates, and set reminders in those calendars so that you are prompted well in advance of those deadlines. You want to allow yourself a time buffer so that if something does blow up, you have time to fix it. As we mention in other areas of this book, asking for deadline extensions or additional time for your project will put you and your professor in an awkward position. Avoid doing this, if you can, by setting earlier deadlines so you and your group members have time to rework or edit parts of the project that might not be as strong as you were hoping. The key here is that everyone needs to be as flexible and as understanding as possible. Let your group members know well in advance if you are going to be unavailable or out of town. Let them know immediately if a problem comes up; do not wait until the last minute or when the problem becomes a crisis. Try not to miss meetings without contacting your colleagues well in advance; you want to show them the same courtesy you would expect to receive. Your colleagues will appreciate you being upfront and thoughtful through the life of the project.

- *Decide on logistics.* What websites or software will you utilize? Have you exchanged emails or telephone numbers? Have you talked about whether everyone has the software or computer access needed to complete the project? Do you need special computer lab time for printing (such as posters, which take much longer to print)? Do you have the supplies you need? Are there costs that need to be shared?

- *Plan and brainstorm ideas.* Get *everyone's* opinion on the substance and direction of the project. Even if people are quiet, call on them and get their opinion. You do not want anyone feeling they are left out or isolated. Getting everyone's opinion cannot only uncover ideas that you may not have thought about, but it can also reveal areas that, after some thought, may not be clear enough. Are there issues or ideas for which your group needs clarification from the professor?

Think about how your group will communicate. In the age of social media, communication seems to be easy; it is right at your fingertips most of the time. But group projects go well beyond just texting someone or sending a message on Facebook. You, your friends, and your classmates have busy schedules. These types of time restrictions necessitate moving beyond sending a quick text about the project. The ideal situation is for your professor to arrange for you to do your group project through a learning management system such as Blackboard, Moodle, or Canvas. These sites have email functions and file management systems that allow your work to be monitored by your professor; if problems arise, the professor can easily see where the problem is. If your professor has not made arrangements for group projects to be done through a learning management system, the group will need to make a decision on how to share and communicate information. One of the most popular ways to do this is through a service such as Google Drive, Evernote, or Dropbox. Communication sites can also help to coordinate messages and files. Some of these include Google Hangouts and Skype.

Collectively review work. You should schedule time for everyone to sit down together and read the work of each student in the group. This exercise serves a couple of useful purposes. It emphasizes the importance of deadlines. It also allows everyone to see the project completely and not just in pieces as individuals send work to each other. It permits multiple edits to be done in a relatively short period.

Stay as upbeat and positive as you can. Working with others means being able to deal with *constructive* criticism. This point is important because editing and providing constructive feedback can be a bit nerve-wracking. Keep in mind that as your colleagues review, critique, and edit your work, their comments are not personal attacks on you! Remember what Michael Corleone said in the movie *The Godfather*—"It's not personal ... it's strictly business." You do not have time to take things personally. Listen to your colleagues' words and see if they are helpful. Engage in a conversation with them about what they are trying to convey. Nerves can be frayed during stressful periods and sometimes *how* someone says something can set off a firestorm. Set aside these issues and focus on *what* they say instead. Try to be as open minded as possible and encourage your colleagues to do the same. Expressing anger through yelling and screaming will only make everyone more frustrated. Think about the long-term objectives you have for the project, and do not worry about how the message is conveyed unless a colleague's attitude and comments are actually hindering progress. That is a problem for you to discuss with your colleagues and possibly with the professor. Meanwhile, maintain a professional approach as you go through each phase of the project.

Communicate with the professor or assistant. If your group finds itself stuck or having disagreements over the direction of the project, talk to the professor! These discussions can be done in two ways: either the full group meets with the professor or a group representative is appointed to speak with the instructor. What is important is that the meeting generates a resolution that is *clearly* communicated to the entire group. If you are having problems or issues with how a particular member of the group is performing on the project, then this meeting with the professor should be discreet and professional. The goal is not to vent frustration, but to resolve particular aspects of the person's behavior that are most detrimental to the project's progress. If you turn this meeting into personal attacks or just whining and complaining, you will not do yourself any favors with your professor. Keep it professional and make sure you convey to the professor that what you are seeking is an outcome to the problem.

Simulations and Virtual Experiences

Simulations have come a long way over the past few decades. Anybody who plays video games knows the power of a simulated setting to teach you to respond to a specific situation and environment in real time. Educators have found ways to transform education using these same tools. At colleges and universities, traditional simulations engage students in one of two ways. The first is through requiring students to play a specific role in a fictional scenario. Common simulations in this category can include Model United Nations, or simulation of a legislature or legislative process (see, for instance, the E-Congress Legislative Policy-Making Exercise [online Congressional simulation] from the University of Virginia's Center for Politics, and the economics simulations of "The Tragedy of the Commons"). These types of simulations are meant to impart information and knowledge about a particular subject or process by making students actually participate in them.

The second type of simulation is based on skill-building exercises that get students to problem-solve and work within groups, much like you would at a job. These types of exercises can include "survival" simulations where you and other group members have to figure out how you might survive on a deserted island or after being stranded on a mountain. Questions like "What you would need for shelter and food?" and "How you would obtain them with limited resources?" force you to put a creative spin on your problem–solving skills.

In assigning class simulations, the professor is certainly not only trying to impart knowledge but also some of the other skills that we discussed, including collaboration, research, and communication skills. Simulations are also based on the tacit acknowledgment that learning can be more effective if it is experiential. Which aspect the professor emphasizes will depend upon the nature, length (some simulations may last for one class period; others may operate for the entire semester), and depth of the simulation being assigned. No matter the nature of the simulation or how long it runs in your class, we have several suggestions that can make this a positive experience for you and your colleagues.

Successfully Navigating a Simulation Activity
✓ Read through every supporting document
✓ Handle group activities like a group project
✓ Stay positive

Read through every supporting document. When the simulation is first assigned, you want to read through every document that has been given to you either in person or online. These documents should describe in great detail how the simulation will work, the objectives of the simulation, what roles people will play, how those roles are chosen, the boundaries and parameters that you have in terms of actions and reactions within the simulation, how you will interact with your colleagues, any related timelines and deadlines, and the final product (paper, response paper, or other results). Do not skip any of these documents; any misunderstandings relating to how the simulation runs and your role in it can have a cascading effect on other participants.

Your simulation may be conducted through simulation software or an online environment. If so, it will probably have a manual to guide you through simulation actions and activities. Read it. If the simulation software or environment does not come with a command "cheat sheet" of commonly used actions and commands, then create one for yourself. Also, make sure you delve into the software or environment as soon as possible. Mistakes made in the online environment can have dire unintended consequences for you and possibly your group. See if you are able to practice commands and functions so that you can assess the effect of each.

Handle group activities like a group project. If your simulation is not computer or online based, then you may be required to engage in group meetings and activities as part of the simulation. You will want to handle these scenarios in much the same way as you would any group project, as we discussed previously. One of the main points of your group meetings should be to develop strategies within the simulation—understanding the simulation scenario and the relationships between all the players and their roles and identifying common game strategies. Simulations can offer an opportunity for a positive experience if everyone engages the activity—if they "get into it"—but a negative approach to the assignment can make it a dreadful experience. Keep focused on the positive elements and the fun of what you are doing in these simulations.

Posters

Posters have become a way for students to learn about a subject in depth while incorporating several practical skills into their repertoire. Posters require significant planning, research, design and, often, presentation by students. Thus, posters have become a useful mechanism to pack a large amount of learning into one assignment. Longer research papers can accompany posters where the poster is the instrument used to summarize the research information.

Across disciplines, conferences have poster sessions where professors and students (both undergraduate and graduate) present their research in poster form. Businesses often utilize posters to summarize information or to make quick project presentations to clients. Thus, skills in developing posters have real world applications.

At the same time, developing clear and coherent posters is not easy and often what we see as poster creators is not what others may see. It is critical that you have your research complete before tackling the poster. You should not see the poster as an opportunity to simply outline your research. A critical eye toward a pleasing aesthetic has to be balanced with critical information. In doing so, there are things that you want to avoid at the outset of your project. Justin Matthews of California State University, Monterey Bay's department

---

The Sad Six of Poster Presentations
- ✗ Unorganized
- ✗ Cluttered
- ✗ Extremely confusing to those outside your field of study
- ✗ Superfluous text
- ✗ Posters without flare
- ✗ Embarrassing to your colleagues or your school

of psychology, refers to these as "the sad six" that constitute "horrible posters" (Matthews, n.d.):

Unorganized. If your poster does not have a good, logical flow, your audience will be lost with regard to the message you are trying to convey.

Cluttered. Your poster should be easy to follow and not filled with lots of distractions or hard-to-read text.

Extremely confusing to those outside your field of study. You want to make your research and the poster understandable to people who are not "experts" in the area you are researching. They should not have to guess at what you are trying to convey.

Superfluous text. You have limited space on your poster. Do not fill it with unnecessary or redundant text. As Dr. Matthews points out, you will be talking to people about your poster (either formally or informally); it should not be a chore for them to follow your discussion and the poster.

Posters without flare. As Dr. Matthews points out, "Posters without pictures suck; they're boring...." While you do not want your entire poster to be filled with pictures, some pictures, graphs, and charts can help make your point in fewer words than you might be able to write. Give your poster some eye appeal, but do not overdo it.

Embarrassing to your colleagues or your school. You probably worked hard on your research and you want to make the best professional impression you can, whether it is in front of a classroom or at a conference. Make sure that your poster is not a last minute mess. These projects consume time and cannot be rushed, particularly in the final stages of production when you need to print the posters (this can take quite a while depending on your printing service, so plan accordingly).

There are *many, many, many* good sources on doing poster presentations on the Internet, but it can be a bit frustrating when some recommend things others say to avoid. Our purpose here is to boil down some of these sites' suggestions into some basic advice, so we have included several poster creation sites in our Web Links section at the end of the chapter. Take a close look at the resources as they can help you kickstart a good poster presentation.

A particularly good source for designing your poster is the University of Texas at Austin's Guide to Creating Research Posters (see the Web Links at the end of the chapter). This guide presents basic tips and ideas about posters, some of which we will look at here. Its authors also have a great webpage containing sample posters and an assessment of the strengths and weaknesses of each. We can think of each element of a poster as content-driven or aesthetic-driven.

Important Elements of a Poster Project
- ✓ Content-driven elements
  - ▪ Research question and why it is important
  - ▪ Research strategy
  - ▪ Summary of your answer
  - ▪ Results of your research
- ✓ Aesthetic-driven elements
  - ▪ Size limitations
  - ▪ Required templates
  - ▪ Presentation type

Content-Driven Elements

Your poster should have the question your research is trying to address, why it is important, your research strategy, a summary of your answer, and the results of your research. Your research question should be immediately visible to your readers so that they know what your poster is about and why they should care (this should be discussed with your professor beforehand).

Your research has to be presented so that a layperson (someone not familiar with your topic) can follow the flow and logic of your research. Even so, organizing your ideas can be daunting, particularly if you are trying to fit a large amount of research onto your poster. Think of your research as a story and your poster as a plot summary. You want your reader to be able to get the plot in just a few short minutes, so what you choose to put on the poster and in what order you present it must be carefully considered. You need to take your poster reader step by step through what may be a large amount of information and work that you have done. So, the flow is important.

Edinburgh Napier University's suggestions for good poster presentations divide content into two types with suggested formats for each. They suggest that if you are reporting on research, you may want to consider the following types of content headings:

1. Title
2. Introduction
3. Methods (how did you conduct your study)
4. Results
5. Discussion
6. Conclusion
7. References

If your poster is focused on a solution to a problem (or policy issue for the social sciences), the content might have these headings:

1. Title
2. Background
3. Definition of problem
4. Possible solutions
5. Rationale for choice of solution
6. Implementation
7. Evaluation

These section headings are meant to give you a sense of ways to organize your information. Regardless of the section headings, remember your poster has limited space, so you need to make sure the text you use is precise and concise.

Aesthetic-Driven Elements

Just as important as the content of your poster is its appearance. The appearance of your poster is critical because if the poster's appearance is distracting, the message you are conveying can be lost. The University of Texas at Austin's Guide to Creating Research Posters has a couple of examples of "bad" posters and what they might look like if the poster's appearance were given a makeover. So what do you need to think about?

First, the size of your poster can determine how your poster may look. If this project is for class, ask your professor if they have a preference for how big the poster should be. If your poster will be presented publicly (such as at a conference), you will want to check for special rules and for how much space will be available. The website PosterPresentations.com has a variety of examples of poster sizes and formats for just about every imaginable scenario. They also have free templates that you can use if your college or university does not have a preferred template for you to use. You should check with your professor to see if your college or university requires you to use one of their specific templates for public presentations or any college or university specific logos that may be needed for the poster.

Beyond the template, a few rules and design ideas should be kept in mind as you construct your poster.

- *Not every bit of white space on the poster needs to be covered!* White space helps viewers read your poster more easily. In the same vein, try to avoid distracting background colors that make your text difficult to read. For example, you want to avoid dark backgrounds with light text, which can be distracting to your audience.

- *Keep sections organized and spaced evenly so that people can easily move through your presentation.*
- *Text should be limited.* Edinburgh Napier University has suggested that a poster should have between 300 and 800 words, with 300 being on the light side, leaving plenty of room for graphics, and 800 being more text intensive.
- *Big is beautiful!* Remember that people will be reading your poster from a distance and that you will be printing on a big piece of poster board (not a regular sheet of paper). You want your fonts to be big enough to catch someone's attention. Likewise, you want the text inside your graphics to also be legible from a distance. Dr. Justin Matthews has suggested these font sizes to make your presentation noticeable:

Poster Title	96 point
Author	48 point
Section Headings	36 point
Text	24 point

Left or fully justify your text so that it has a neat appearance.
- *Use clear fonts.* The standbys are always good—Times New Roman, Helvetica, Arial, and so on. You want your fonts to be professional and consistent. Different fonts can be used to highlight important things such as quotes (but remember that *too* many fonts can be distracting).
- *Graphics are needed.* Graphics can pack much information into a small bit of space. Graphics, including the type that you use inside the graphics, should be visible and clear from a distance. If you are going to use graphics from the Internet, you need to be aware of the quality of the graphic or picture. These should be at a resolution of at least 300 dpi, but higher is better, as you want them to be sharp when they print on your poster. You also need to provide appropriate citations and credits for any graphics that are not yours. You can find plenty of free and copyright-free graphics online through such sites as WikiCommons and FreeImages.

The final item you want to pay attention to with posters is how the poster is to be presented. If you are making a class presentation of the poster, your professor will likely have guidelines on how the poster should be presented. If you are presenting this poster in a professional setting (such as a job presentation or at a professional academic conference), other details become important. When people approach you and your poster, greet them politely and with enthusiasm for your topic. Let them know that you would be happy to answer any questions they have (even if you are nervous and would rather bolt for the door!). Give them a few minutes to read through the poster. Some people might read the poster and move along to the next one. In other cases, the viewer may want to engage you in a discussion but has no interest in reading through the poster. This discussion is an opportunity to make an impression upon someone—a future colleague, graduate professor, or a research partner. You never know whom you might run into at these types of presentations. So talk to them about your poster, but do not read your poster to them. Talk to them about issues and dynamics that are not on the poster so that you keep them engaged with the material.

Oral Presentations[1]

There is probably no better skill for your education or career than oral communication skills. We often suggest that our own students take one or two classes on the topic as a way of getting more formalized training in the finer points of things like debate, speech-making, and professional presentations. Why? First, practicing different types of speaking can make any oral presentation easier over time. Likewise, you will also practice outlining, research, organization of ideas, and shaping messages for different audiences—all skills that can be used in numerous assignments and scenarios. Few people are "naturally talented" at giving presentations that are professional yet engaging. How many times have you sat in a classroom where the presenter (instructor or student) was putting the class to sleep and you were trying to find a way to tunnel out of the room? Your first presentation will offer you a sense of the difficulty in giving good oral presentations, but the idea here is to give you some advice to make that first presentation easier. Remember, oral presentations are a skill you are trying to acquire and hone over time. Do not avoid them, because you need to practice this skill that can help you throughout your life.

Types of Oral Presentations

Oral presentations can take many forms. They can range from small briefings where you present a quick overview of a subject to detailed presentations of formal research you conduct for your class. Hampden-Sydney College's Ferguson Center for Public Speaking divides presentations into two types: informative speaking and persuasive speaking. Informative speaking has as its goal presenting information to your audience. In your classes, these presentations may often be associated with the presentation of your research on a particular topic or the presentation of a longer semester project or even a group project. Persuasive speaking is meant to enforce an opinion or change an opinion

....

1 Co-authored with Amy Pason, Department of Communication Studies, University of Nevada, Reno.

(Brydon & Scott, 2008). These presentations may be associated with presenting particular viewpoints, public policy debates and discussions, current events, criticisms, or advocacy for a cause. Thus, one of the first things you want to do is to figure out what type of presentation your professor wants to see in the classroom. The type of presentation will determine how you proceed in constructing and delivering it.

As a social science student you may be asked to give numerous types of speeches, but the following suggestions generally apply to all of them:

- *Be aware of the time limit.* Make sure to narrow your topic to best address it in the time allotted for the speech.
- *Direct your speech to a mixed audience* (those with expertise in your area and those that might be laypeople or not as informed about the topic).
- *Be prepared to adapt to your audience.* Give attention to what you are presenting but also be aware of how your audience is receiving it. If there are several puzzled looks, try to clarify some of your points or ask if there are questions you need to address.
- *Avoid technical or highly specialized terms.* If you use them, make sure to define or find other ways to clarify them for the audience.
- *Think of your speech (from introduction to end) as a story.* Listeners can learn and stay engaged—even through the more complex areas.

Organizing and Preparing Your Speech

After researching your topic, you should create an outline for your speech ideas— you want to give yourself enough information to cue your memory or reference specific details of sources and evidence, but not so much that you end up memorizing your speech. An outline is also the easiest tool to revise, edit, change the order of items as you practice, and find how your information "flows best" during the presentation. You are looking to put your ideas into direct, concise sentences: What exactly am I going to explain? What exactly do I want to argue? The outline helps you ensure you have ample support for each main topic or argument, as you can visually see the number of supporting pieces of evidence and how that evidence fits together or progresses to make your argument.

For example, you may *claim,* "Many refugees are coming to the United States from Central America." You have to provide *evidence* for this claim: In the last fiscal year, nearly 70,000 children traveling without their parents were apprehended by border agents. Most of these children came from El Salvador, Guatemala, and Honduras. In 2014, 2,300 applied for refugee status according to the State Department (Foley, 2015).

Most speeches should strive for 3–5 main topics or arguments. These overarching topics can be broken down into subtopics/claims—again, grouping or focusing on 2–3 subtopics per area. This "grouping" of ideas gives audiences (and yourself) manageable chunks of information to remember, and also ensures you are stating your topics/claims as specifically as possible to directly relate and connect to the evidence or supporting information provided.

Include All Speech Parts

All speeches should include an introduction, body, and conclusion. *Introductions* should include an *attention getter* (e.g., stories, quotes, etc.) appropriate to the topic to start the speech confidently and pique the audience's interest. You also want to build a relationship with your audience by providing some *orientation information* (Sprague, Stuart, & Bodary, 2015). Such information establishes your credibility and explains why your information should matter to your audience. It "eases" the audience into the topic by providing essential background information, thus preparing them to understand the general direction of the topic.

The introduction should also include your thesis statement (your main argument) and a preview of your main points. These give your audience a road map of what will come in the speech—remember, your speech is not a secret and you are not Sherlock Holmes waiting until the end for the "big reveal." You want your audience to follow with you as you present this information, not to be guessing ahead.

In the *body of the speech*, you should present an organized discussion of your topics and evidence. In doing so, be sure to cite sources as you present. It is also helpful to signal when you are changing topics as well by transitioning and linking one topic to the next. Phrases like "My second point ..." or "Next, I would like to discuss ..." are appropriate to let your audience know you are moving on to the next major point of your presentation.

As with the introduction, the *conclusion* should provide closure and signal that the speech is ending. You may want to provide a summary of the main topics/arguments presented, to restate the main thesis, and to reconnect your topic logically with a larger context by showing the broader implications for the information you have provided. In some speeches you might make an appeal or call to action. *Do not* include new arguments or information in the conclusion—this is unsettling and does not help with "closure" for the audience. Finally, the conclusion should end memorably. Just as you started with an attention getter, end on a definitive note. There is nothing worse than ending and having the audience unsure if you are finished! Make sure that the ending is also something that fits into the context of what you have done in the presentation. You do not want to end a presentation on the problem of family divorce with "And now, an interpretive dance ..." (although that may be memorable!).

Delivering Your Presentation (Without Throwing Up)

Almost everyone gets some form of presentation anxiety before the presentation. It is natural because all eyes are on you. Many people avoid giving speeches because it tends to make them uncomfortable and "nervous." Nerves are experienced by even the best speakers—and can be managed. We get anxious when there are "new" situations or when we are unsure of outcomes. The more you make speaking routine and see public speaking as "just another day at the office," the less panicky you will feel. If you cannot get rid of your anxiety, the best thing is to use it to your advantage or learn to control it.

How Not to Throw Up during Your Presentation
✓ Know your material
✓ Remember people will not see how nervous you are
✓ Control your "extra" energy

Know your material. Practicing what you will say, talking through your speech with a friend, or even pretending to answer questions in an interview will help you develop the brain "muscle memory" to be ready to present. Do not expect the speech to come out the same every time you present—the goal is to present material clearly, not to have a memorized script. If you forget a small point or a piece of evidence, that's okay! The audience may never know. Likewise, you should never read your presentation word for word from a prepared manuscript. This process will cause problems and, frankly, will bore your audience. Likewise, never start any presentation with anything other than an appropriate word. Starting with "ummm" or "ahhhh" conveys you do not know what you are doing up there right now. Have confidence and express yourself with a solid opening.

Remember people will not see how nervous you are. Unless you have very overt nervous tells (playing with your hair or pulling up your shirt during the *whole* speech), people will not know you are nervous. (Unless, of course, you tell them—and they really do not need to know that!) Focus more on getting your message out, and those nerves will be the last thing on your mind. You may not have confidence, but as Aaron Sorkin once wrote in the television series *The West Wing*, "Act as if ye have faith, and faith shall be given to you. To put it another way, fake it till you make it."

Control your "extra" energy (what we see as nerves). Practice good, tall posture (to allow yourself to take in deep breaths); take a few deep, slow, calming breaths to reduce anxiety; and even clench and release your fists to reduce any shaking or excess energy. Keep your feet planted on the floor (no dancing or standing like a flamingo)—all of this will give you the sense that you are in control and those nerves will go away.

In delivering your presentation, there are a number of techniques that can help ensure a smooth delivery. There is *never* a good reason to memorize or read your speech word for word. Some call this "zombie" delivery because you do not interact with your audience and you really don't even notice that you have an audience at all as you are following (probably monotonously) the script you have memorized or are reading (Vrooman, 2015). The preferred delivery method is called extemporaneous speaking: you prepare and practice (often a key sentence or key word outline) before you present, but it is up to you to explain in your own conversational and natural way the ideas following the plan and focus of your outline. The audience is looking to hear from you, rather than listen to something they could have read on their own.

There are several benefits to not sticking to the script with a memorized manuscript. Natural, conversational speaking style helps your audience understand and retain information. You will tend to use shorter, more direct sentences, naturally elaborate and explain connections between ideas, and provide natural signposts (first, I'll talk about ...)—all things that help your audience follow and easily understand what you are discussing. This speaking style also allows you to interact with the audience. Maybe you can reference or relate your topic to what previous speakers have said. Maybe you can give examples directly related to members of the audience. Maybe you can "go off plan" and explain terminology that might be confusing to the audience (once you see the quizzical looks on their faces). Finally, speaking extemporaneously shows that you are a confident speaker. You are more likely to have good posture and relaxed body language, employ natural gestures, and make eye contact. If you are not stuck reading notes on a lectern, you can also move strategically around the room—moving and stopping for each point to visually show your audience when you are heading to the next topic.

Using Visual Aids in Presentations

There is never a good reason to display your speech word for word on a PowerPoint or other presentational software, and there are very few situations where visual aids are needed in a presentation. A visual aid should be just that: aiding and adding to your speech, not taking it over entirely. The attention should be on you, the speaker. The speaker should be able to carry on with the speech even if there is a technical failure.

If you do use visuals, here are some points to keep in mind. Make sure you have practiced with the technology you will be using. You do not want to keep your audience waiting because you do not know how to operate the computer or projector that will display your visual aids. Make your visuals polished and professional by using fonts and a background that are large enough for the audience to read and limit the amount of information on the slide. Do not overuse animations, slide transitions, or sound effects, as they are distracting and unnecessary.

If you should limit the number of visuals, when are they most helpful? Visuals help audiences understand more complex materials, like definitions of concepts or terms or graphs to represent statistical data. An outline of your talk at the beginning can also help your audience understand what you will be covering in the presentation.

Over time, you will develop a style that works for you. If you notice from your professors and others that you have seen give public lectures or speeches, each person has a different style, a different way of connecting with the audience, a different way to make their point. Practice has allowed these speakers to get to the point they are at. When watching speakers, ask yourself what these speakers are doing correctly and what they are doing incorrectly. Learn from the good and not so good—what you want to do and what you may not want to do. Eventually, you will build your own style that works for you and your audiences.

Important Points to Remember

- ✓ Much (but not all) of college is about honing marketable career skills
- ✓ Most of those skills will be built doing course projects of one kind or another—understanding which skills you are supposed to be developing in each one is critical
- ✓ Understand the parameters and expectations of each project
- ✓ Be especially organized and professional in group projects
- ✓ When presenting orally or in a poster, know which elements to include (or exclude), organize those elements carefully, and *practice!*

Bibliography

Brydon, S. R., & Scott, M. D. (2008). *Between one and many: The art and science of public speaking.* New York: McGraw-Hill Higher Education.

Dougherty, J.E., & Pfaltzgraff, R.L. (2001). *Contending theories of international relations: A comprehensive survey* (5th ed.). New York: Longman.

Foley, E. (2015, July 15). More than 2,000 Central Americans applied for refugee status to come to the US. Retrieved from http://www.huffingtonpost.com/entry/

more-than-2000-central-americans-applied-for-refugee-status-to-come-to-the-
us_us_55a6d829e4b0896514d04983

Matthews, J. (n.d.). Poster guide. Retrieved from http://justinlmatthews.com/
posterhelp/posterguide/

National Association of Colleges and Employers. (2012, December 7). Job outlook: The
candidate skills/qualities employers want. Retrieved from http://www.sjsu.edu/
careercenter/docs/job-outlook-survey-NACE_2012.pdf

Sprague, J., Stuart, D., & Bodary, D. (2015). *The speaker's handbook*. Boston: Cengage
Learning.

Vrooman, S. (2015). *The zombie guide to public speaking: 2nd "dead"ition*. Steven Vrooman.

Web Links

No! We did not get paid for mentioning any of
these (we wish!). We are not click bait suppliers!

Dropbox: https://www.dropbox.com/

E-Congress Legislative Policy-Making Exercise [online Congressional simulation] from
the University of Virginia's Center for Politics: http://www.centerforpolitics.org/
yli.html

Evernote: https://evernote.com/

FreeImages: http://www.freeimages.com/

Google Drive: https://www.google.com/drive/

Google Hangouts: https://talkgadget.google.com/

Impress: https://www.libreoffice.org/discover/impress/

Learning and Loving Earth Science: Tragedy of the Commons Fisheries Management
Simulation Game, an Educational Resource: http://es.earthednet.org/fishing-game

Microsoft PowerPoint Online: https://office.live.com/start/PowerPoint.aspx

National Model United Nations: http://www.nmun.org/

Prezi: https://prezi.com

Skype: https://www.skype.com/en/

University of North Carolina at Chapel Hill. Literature Reviews—The Writing
Center: http://writingcenter.unc.edu/handouts/literature-reviews/

University of Texas at Austin's Guide to Creating Research Posters: https://www.
utexas.edu/ugs/our/poster

WikiCommons: https://commons.wikimedia.org/wiki/Main_Page

CHAPTER 5

CAN YOU GOOGLE THAT?

Where to Find Information[1]

When your professor assigns your project, you inevitably have to go find the information you need. Information technology has revolutionized the gathering of information and the way in which it can be presented to you. Students are living through one of the greatest information revolutions since Johannes Gutenberg's printing press (around 1440; yeah, it's been that long). The revolution has democratized information, providing students and researchers with rapid and generally easy access. It has also democratized the production of information so that anyone can do it. This brave new world has both positives and negatives. The positive side is that information can come from sources to which we may not otherwise have access. For instance, first-hand accounts of a revolution on a blog or through Twitter can provide insight that you may not see in a news report or an academic paper. But this raises important questions: How reliable is that information? How informed is the source? On the negative side, there may be too much information. How can students deal with information overload and sift through the abundance to find the most reliable sources? The core concerns that every modern student must now address relate to (a) how to find the right information and (b) how to determine its reliability.

Let's start with the basics of how to find information. Every discipline in the social sciences has its own collection of sources that students and professors access for research, and we will get to some of those collections a bit later. More fundamental is how to get help from professionals. So there's this person called a librarian at your college or university. We say this a bit tongue in cheek, but we, and probably many other professors, routinely have students tell us

1 Much of the content of this chapter has been co-authored with Rudy Leon, Associate Director, Library Research Services & Learning Spaces, University of North Carolina, Wilmington.

"I can't find any information on my topic." It's at this point our age starts to show, and we tell incomprehensible stories about trudging through book stacks and sifting through indexes to find information. At the same time, without being a bit tongue in cheek, we have also met students who never had a librarian at their high school because of budget cuts. It is therefore important to convey the importance of librarians to your project. Realistically, it is rarely, if ever, that you have identified a topic about which absolutely no one has ever written. So when we hear "I can't find any information on my topic," our first thought is that the search for information was somehow lacking.

The librarians at your college or university have gone through years of training in library sciences, and through this training they have mastered the art of retrieving information. Large libraries will have discipline-specific research librarians whose primary job is to help students and faculty find information for their research topics. Smaller libraries may have librarians that serve multiple academic departments, but will still be familiar with how to find information across those disciplines. If you are absolutely lost when beginning the search on your research topic, your first step should be to contact a subject or reference librarian. While your professor can make suggestions about sources for your project, subject librarians will have access to a full range of tools to make your research much more productive.

Researchers have studied how students interact with subject librarians and how those librarians can help students. These studies reveal that building a solid relationship with your subject or reference librarian can benefit you for your entire academic career. Librarians are research superheroes with a wealth of information on your research topic and on a host of related subjects. They can provide important skills and services that you probably won't be able to find anywhere else on your campus (Magi & Mardeusz, 2013). The following are just a subset of what they can do for you.

Librarians Can Show You How To
- ✓ Find and use reference sources
- ✓ Synthesize information
- ✓ Use library procedures and resources
- ✓ Find details about the specific projects on which you are working
- ✓ Develop your topic and research
- ✓ Clarify research
- ✓ Exploit their research experience
- ✓ Find important campus people
- ✓ Use citation information
- ✓ Use technical assistance

Provide knowledge about reference sources and their effective use. This means not just having knowledge of research resources and databases, but also related issues such as framing a question for effective Internet and database searches and using advanced research techniques and tools hidden inside databases.

Help synthesize that information. The research involved in answering any student's questions may involve obtaining information from a wide range of sources or finding information deeply hidden within sources. Librarians have the skills and the background to bring this information together.

Offer knowledge of library procedures and resources. This includes accessing items from remote storage and archives and conducting interlibrary loans for access to resources owned by other libraries.

Find details about the specific projects on which you are working. They may be familiar with your professor and, because they have worked on the same projects with other students in previous terms, they may know specifically what your professor is looking for.

Help to develop your topic and research. Librarians spend much time understanding who produces the best sources of information, the kinds of information available, and the viability of a research topic given the availability of information.

Clarify research. In addition to developing your topic with you, librarians can often help clarify what you are trying to get at in your research. Through a discussion with your librarian, you can hone and sharpen your research question, goals, and objectives. Sometimes it is good to talk to a person who is familiar with your area of research but is also removed enough to ask questions objectively, so that you can see the layers and complexities in your topic.

Exploit their research experience for your benefit. You may not realize it, but librarians at colleges and universities are often part of the faculty and earn tenure and promotion based not just on service to students and faculty, but on their publication record as well. So they have plenty of research experience that they can draw upon to help you with your research projects.

Find important campus people. Librarians interact with a large number of people on campus. This interaction gives librarians the opportunity to know people who may be of help in your research. Librarians are good at making connections with faculty members who might be able to help formally (such as an advisor or thesis chair) and informally (someone with whom you can talk about your topic).

Assist with citations. During your time at college or university, you will take courses across several disciplines that each have their own way of citing information. It is up to you to conform to those standards. Some professors will be extremely picky about this; others may just want you to be consistent with the style you use. Librarians are familiar with all the citation formats that you may need to use in your career. They will be able to help with each discipline's nuances and formats for citing material. Their services can be really useful when you are doing research for multiple courses. If your research is being presented outside the classroom, librarians can keep you from running afoul of copyright law and within fair use and licensing agreements for using videos, photos, and text from sources that are not your own.

Offer technical assistance. Some librarians can be helpful with the technical aspects of your research such as formatting posters, word processing problems (your information technology center can be helpful here as well), data or spreadsheet issues, and even audio and video issues with your PowerPoint presentations. When it is crunch time, your librarians can be lifesavers in these areas!

After discussing research strategy, questions, and approaches with a subject librarian, what should you do next? Look for specific sources of information on your topic. There are some simple sources that are easily overlooked and, oddly enough, one of the most overlooked sources of information today is a book on your topic.

Students may bypass books for a host of reasons: they are doing research late when the library might not be open, they do not relish lugging heavy books to and from the library, or books may seem to be another form of information overload. But this is a shortsighted strategy. Books provide both a general overview of a topic and in many cases a detailed treatment of a topic. They can provide the necessary background for your research, and particular books may be considered foundational to understanding your area of research; not including them in your analysis may give your professor reason to question how well you have done your research. Just as importantly, books can be a great source to use in finding other articles or books—just look in the back at the bibliography and you will usually find a wealth of information that can key you in to the important research on the book's topic. Keep in mind also that many libraries are encouraging the use of eBooks; so lugging books from the library is getting a bit easier.

Of course, the standard source of information for many of the social sciences has become the online database. These are convenient (hey, research from home and at any time!) and generally have authoritative sources. It is also true that these can be extremely expensive sources for your library to maintain, with complicated annual subscriptions that can cost tens of thousands of dollars or more, depending on the database and the number of users. You should consult with your subject librarian about which of the many databases may be appropriate for your research. Some databases may be obvious—students in the social sciences use the Social Science Citation Index, JSTOR, and EBSCO Academic Search Premier quite frequently. ProQuest has separate databases for social sciences generally, and individually for political science, sociology, congressional research, and statistical abstracts. However, there is a world of specialized databases out there that can make your research paper sing with information.

For instance, students doing research on race relations in the US might find the database *Black Freedom Struggle in the 20th Century* useful, as it contains a wealth of historical and government information on the civil rights movement. Students doing research on gender issues may find *GenderWatch* useful, as it covers articles and news surrounding gender issues. But it is also the case that the nature of social science research is cross-disciplinary. Learning about non-social science databases could prove to be useful in cases where your topic crosses disciplinary boundaries. Students working in the area of health care policies may find articles from PubMed (a medical journal database) quite handy. Students doing work in the area of international law may find Westlaw or LexisNexis useful for case research. (Though legal databases are often quite restrictive about who can use them. If you are not a member of a law school, you may need to check with your subject librarian about access to these specialized databases.)

Finding Data

Social science research is often empirically based, whether in the form of detailed case studies or complex models driven by numerical data. After discussing your class project with your professor and settling on a research question (what social science question or policy you are trying to examine), you will need to find evidence to support your argument. Research at the undergraduate level in the social sciences generally falls into two categories: case studies (using qualitative methods) and quantitative models (depending upon your courses and your background). Case studies examine a particular topic or subject in detail using qualitative research methods such as interviews, surveys, field observations, primary document analysis, and secondary sources such as journal articles and books. These types of data collection methods should be discussed with your professor to gauge the level of detail required. Does the professor want to see, for instance, interviews with people? Is your research part of an internship or exchange where travel could be required? Is your professor seeking to give you experience with primary sources such as diaries, government documents, or manuscripts? Or is your professor expecting you to use mainly secondary sources (books and articles) for your case studies? These are the types of questions you want to ask before you go about collecting data that may not be very useful. Once you determine the scope of your case study, it is best to then sit down with (guess who) your subject librarian so that you can determine the availability of primary and secondary sources.

If travel or interviews are required, your professor should provide guidance on how they should be done, if at all. If you are unfamiliar with these types of research, Purdue University's Online Writing Lab (OWL) has a great primer on how to prepare for primary research such as interviews, survey research, observational analysis, and the analysis of primary documents.

For students who will be receiving training in policy analysis, social statistics, econometrics, psychometrics, or other types of quantitative analysis, the primary method to investigate your question may be through numerical data. Depending upon your skill level and the training you receive in your class, you may be using data for some basic descriptive analysis or for more complex models. The nature of your analysis is something, again, that you need to assess with your professor in the context of your research topic. The transformation of data collection techniques in just the past few years has opened up new frontiers in social science data. Each discipline in the social sciences has data sources and repositories that students and professors often rely upon. For instance, in sociology, you can find links to sociology data at the American Sociological Association's data website. In political science, the Inter-university Consortium for Political and Social Research (ICPSR) has been the flagship website for researchers to deposit their data sets. More generally, there is also the Registry of Research Data Repositories that provides a searchable database of repositories for research data. The website is multidisciplinary and covers a wide range of research areas from chemistry to psychology, with the major social sciences included. Start with the browse menu to look through the data available for your subject discipline. Those who might be doing research using US federal government data should check out the US government's open data website that contains data released by the US government. For those doing research using Canadian government data, the Statistics Canada website offers the same data access for students.

Students in the social sciences may find their research focuses on another country or across multiple countries (this is usually referred to as cross-sectional or cross-national research). Obtaining data for countries has become easier thanks to several websites maintained by international organizations. The United Nations (UN) maintains a data portal that can connect to more than 30 different databases maintained by UN agencies. UNData provides open access to databases across countries (where you can obtain data for individual countries) and specialized topical databases that include data and information on topics such as HIV/AIDS, education, environment and climate change, agriculture, gender, health, populations, refugees, and trade. The most comprehensive database of socio-economic and political indicators can be found at the World Bank's World Development Indicators website. These data are collected from the national government members of the World Bank and contain more than

1,300 variables. All these sites have interfaces that allow you to select your variables and the countries and years for the data.

A bit of caution should be used with all these data websites. These websites are large and they can take some time to navigate. Some are a bit complicated in terms of accessing the data. Make sure that you do not wait until the last moment to try to download your data for analysis. You should talk to your subject librarian if you are having trouble navigating these websites. It is also the case that some libraries may have data librarians on staff who are versed in being able to find and download data. Check to see if your library has a data librarian who might be able to assist you.

The analysis of your data can be done with several software packages. You will want to check with your university or college's information technology representatives to see which are available to you. Common statistical packages used in the social sciences include Stata, SPSS, Minitab, and R, and your professor may prefer one over the others. Most data can be downloaded into formats that are compatible with your software program. If you do not have much experience with statistical packages, basic statistical analysis can be completed in a simple spreadsheet program like Excel, which can produce basic statistics and graphs of data. If you do not know how to use software such as Excel, which is part of the Microsoft Office Suite, you may be able to find on-campus resources that provide cheat sheets and tutorials on how to use these tools. Your university or college may also be a subscriber to Lynda.com, which is an online video training website with hundreds of tutorials on a variety of subjects from how to create websites to how to use specific software packages.

One of the key problems that students have with software is that they do not take the time to actually learn how to use it correctly or completely. Taking the time to go through a tutorial for MS Office, for instance, will provide you with tools in managing footnotes in research papers, tables of contents, heading and subheading formats, inserting citations, transferring information into your presentation software, and other useful shortcuts and hints that can save you *hours* of time.

How to (and How Not to) Find Information

While much of what we discussed above deals with general services that librarians are capable of providing, their primary function is to help you find information. Some are going to be better than others at this function, and you may have to talk to a few librarians to maximize your research findings. That's okay because not everyone is going to be familiar with your research. So give yourself a bit of time to work with the library staff to get the maximum benefit. At the same time, if you come to a librarian the day before your research is due, do not expect miracles, especially during busy times like midterms and finals.

> **How Librarians Can Help You Find Information**
> ✓ Refining and honing your research question
> ✓ Translating your research question into searchable terms for databases and the Internet
> ✓ Helping with advanced search techniques
> ✓ Identifying the types of resources needed

Refining and honing your research question. Professors are good at helping you to identify your research question, but translating that across disciplines or into smaller, more manageable parts is not always easy. Librarians are good at helping you break down your research question into component parts that can be easier to tackle than the one big research question. In doing so, they will also be able to identify a range of resources that might otherwise have been overshadowed by the larger research question. A research question that deals with how group leaders make decisions may turn up the usual studies in political science and business on how leaders make decisions. But if you dissect that topic a bit more, you will find that psychologists have done considerable research on how and why leaders make the decisions they do. This research can add a different dimension of understanding that you may not have had before refining and breaking down the broader topic.

Translating your research question into searchable terms for databases and the Internet. While we will cover database and Internet searches in more detail a bit later, for now remember that librarians can provide support in breaking up your research question into searchable terms that can narrow down a mountain of information into something much more manageable.

Helping with advanced search techniques. Librarians are experts at limiting results, finding alternative terminology (thesaurus terms) for a topic (e.g., capital punishment vs. execution vs. death penalty), using complex Boolean searches to include and exclude terminology, and alternative strategies for difficult or archaic subject matter. (We will go through some of the common research search strategies below.)

Identifying the types of resources needed. Once you have your research question, librarians are helpful in identifying the type of resources you may need— newspaper, data, scholarly, books, statistics, white papers, primary sources, or government reports. They can also be quite helpful in identifying databases or other sources containing that kind of information and how to search the sources for that information.

As we said previously, the information revolution has produced "information overload" for many people; so much information can actually be paralyzing. Some day you may find yourself with 50 articles and 20 books in front of you and only a hot cup of coffee to keep you awake. It makes for an interesting selfie, but it can be stressful and sometimes counterproductive. The question becomes how you can make your searches more effective by isolating only the information you really need. This question is not just a matter of making the information easier for you to find. You have to think in a practical sense—you are busy! You need to get at information in the most efficient way possible. If you have research projects due in four classes, you have to use your time wisely. You do not want to type a bunch of words into a search engine and hope what pops up is good enough. You have to have a *search strategy* to make your searches work for you and not against you.

There are two places to begin your search for information. The first is the library databases and the second is the Internet. Library databases should be your first stop in doing research. First, subject librarians will point you to them as a place that, usually, has the most authoritative research done on the topic. Second, it is a controlled search environment, meaning that subject librarians know the best way to get results for you if you find you need help.

Library search engines and databases are hierarchically structured so that information is cataloged for easy searching. This structure means that information is cataloged under a subject heading and research is tagged with that subject heading, making it easy to retrieve. While every database is different in terms of how it catalogs its information (your subject librarian can help with how a particular database may use subject headings), it is worth taking a look at one example. We can use the EBSCO Academic Search Premier database as an example of a database search using different search strategies. The Reynolds Community College Library (Woetzel, n.d.) provides a good example of a search on a research question that thousands of students have examined—the death penalty.

Suppose that your professor has asked that the project deal with the use of lethal injection methods in carrying out the death penalty (capital punishment) in a state of the United States. The professor has left which state to use in your research up to you. Thirty-three of 50 states of the United States currently allow lethal injection as an option for capital punishment. You have decided to examine Kentucky's use of lethal injection and its practices in carrying it out. The first place to start is to construct a keyword list related to your research question or topic. Your keywords might look like this list:

Death penalty
Capital punishment

Executions
Lethal injection
Kentucky

These are all search words that are relevant or are different ways to refer to the subject of the death penalty. Thinking of alternative terminology can be important. While there is really no substantive difference between the "death penalty" and "capital punishment," they are both popular ways to refer to the same issue. If we do a general text search for the death penalty using the TX *All Text* search option (that will pick up any instance of the words "death" and "penalty" in the text of an article), we get the results shown in Figure 5.1.

Notice that we get more than 37,000 word hits in the database. But realistically that does not help much—we have hit information overload. The search did yield some useful information to us, though. If you look at the area marked as *Subjects*, you find a list of subject headings. The first one is "CAPITAL punishment" and the second one is "EXECUTIONS & executioners." These are subject headings that the database uses to organize the information. We can then search for "capital punishment" using SU *Subject Terms* as the search method. If we repeat the search with "Capital Punishment" as a subject heading, we get a much narrower focus, as Figure 5.2 shows. We have narrowed the focus of the search to more than 7,800 articles that are cataloged under the subject of capital punishment. That is still too many results to be useful, but it is an improvement. Now that we have isolated the subject catalog heading, it may be helpful to get the research narrowed down to a particular facet of capital punishment.

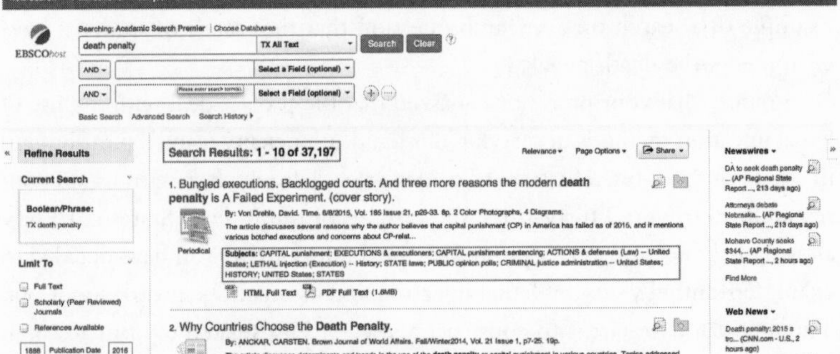

FIGURE 5.1 Death Penalty Text Search

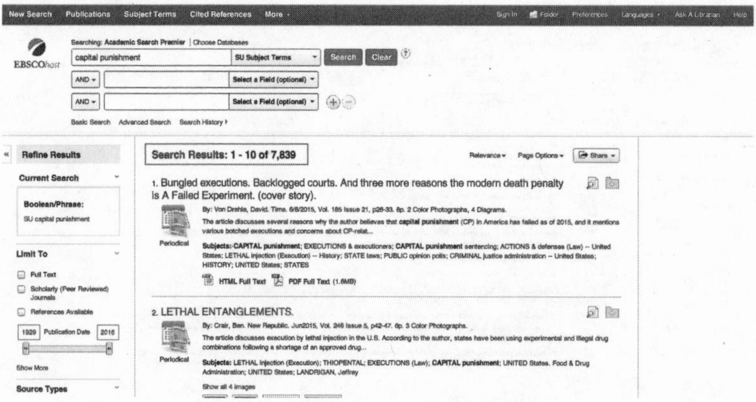

FIGURE 5.2 Capital Punishment Subject Search

If we narrow the subject search down to "capital punishment" and "lethal injection," we then get a considerably lower number of references. As Figure 5.3 shows, we have generated 260 references that include both "capital punishment" and "lethal injection."

This result gives us a much more manageable list, but we can narrow it down still further because we are particularly interested in lethal injection as practiced in the state of Kentucky. So let's add Kentucky as a subject search and view the results. When we do this, as Figure 5.4 shows, we now have a quite reasonable list from which to begin our research, with 13 references that are specific to capital punishment using lethal injection in the state of Kentucky. Notice that the references include information from both periodicals (such

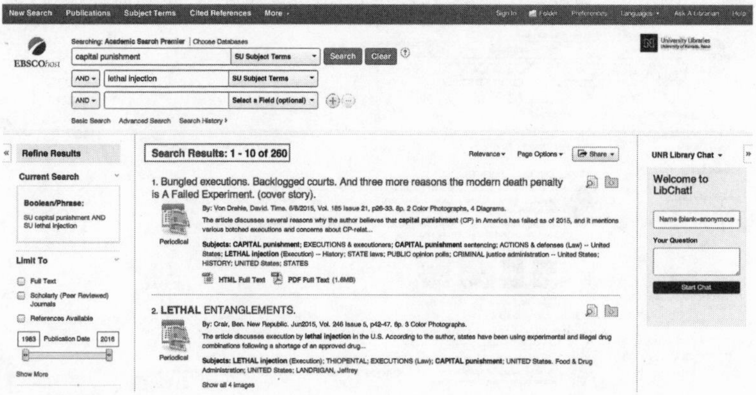

FIGURE 5.3 Lethal Injection Subject Heading

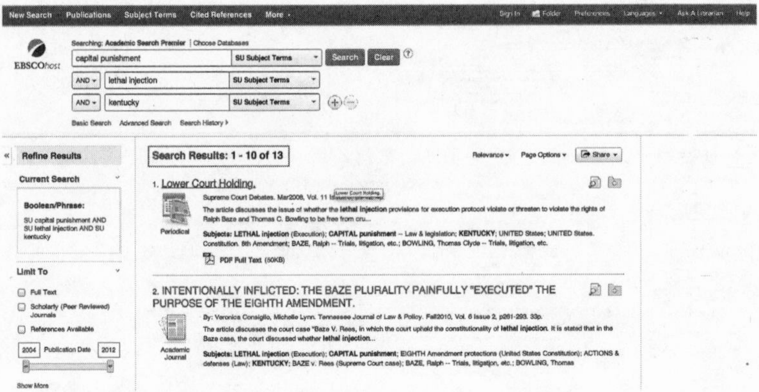

FIGURE 5.4 Kentucky Subject Heading

as magazines) and academic journals (peer-reviewed research). We will talk about the distinction between these shortly, but at this point you have a start that includes a variety of sources to examine.

Let's suppose that these results were a bit too restrictive and that you may need to include references where Kentucky is going to be mentioned in some capacity, but where it may not be the central focus of the article. Some articles may talk about lethal injection, but only use Kentucky as an example while comparing it to others. These could be very helpful to your research. You can change the search strategy to broaden the method of searching by changing Kentucky from SU *Subject Terms* (a cataloged subject heading) to TX *All Text* (a text term) to be searched for in each article. As Figure 5.5 shows, this opens

FIGURE 5.5 Kentucky Text Word Search

up the results a bit to 40 references. This is a solid number of sources but not so many that you could never manage them all.

The death penalty example we just used is an easy example of a quick search strategy that demonstrates how information may be organized in a database. You must keep in mind, though, that information in each database may follow different rules. Reading on a database's help site about how that database is organized and talking with a subject librarian can be of use here to develop strategies that can be more effective, efficient, and productive in your searches. It is also important to point out that each database has other ways to isolate information, so it is important to understand the nuances. Doing so can make your effort much more focused rather than just wading through page after page of information without any structure or direction.

The other obvious area to search for information is the Internet. The Internet has been a remarkable game changer in information technology, but it has many drawbacks for students. The Internet has democratized information both for consumers and for producers. That means two things for students trying to find information. First, we are back to the information overload problem. A topic search of the Internet can bring back thousands, even millions, of pieces of information and research results. Second, because there are few standards and procedures with regard to how authoritative the information is, you, as a student researcher, are left to judge reliability on your own. That is a tough thing to do (even for professors), particularly if you are researching a topic for the first time. Let's deal with each of these problems.

How you access the information, particularly which search engines you use, can influence the results you get. A simple comparison example illustrates the point. We want to get some basic information on the Shona people of Zimbabwe and conduct a simple search of two keywords—*Shona* and *Zimbabwe*. We ran the search across five different search engines (Dogpile.com, Google. com, Yahoo.com, Yandex.com, and Yippy.com) and find that while each search engine produces results in similar ways, there are some important differences. To follow this discussion, open up a web browser window now and create a tab for each of these search engines. Then type *Shona* and *Zimbabwe* into each search field. We will discuss some of these results, comparing how and why they differ.

By virtue of its extensive presence on the Internet, Google is the first search engine that most students use. This makes sense because the folks at Google have incorporated many tools and applications into their web search experience. If you sign up for a Google account (or already have one), you can find a host of useful tools that will enhance your web experience, some useful for your research and organization and some less so. But being the most popular may not make Google the best for a specific task like academic research.

If you look at the results across all five search engines, you will see some commonalities. One of them is that results can be cluttered. On Dogpile. com, the first five links for information are advertisements. It is only on the sixth link that you finally get to the web results you want. From the company's perspective, this makes sense because advertising is how they make their money from a generally free search engine. From a research perspective, the clutter is just junk information to sift through.

Another common characteristic is that the search engines appear to highlight the most popular sites, such as Wikipedia, at the top. This type of result has to do with the algorithm or formulas that the search engine is using to decide how to display the information. Some search engines base their results on the popularity of websites, the relationship the website has to the topic you are researching, or even advertising considerations. Thus, the choice of search engines has an effect on the type of information you receive in your search.

Choice of search engine can affect the number of sites that result from your search. In the case of Google, more than 1.5 million sites were found that have something to do with Shona and Zimbabwe. Certainly that means your search terms are broad, but it also means that the search engine is probably picking up superfluous information as well. There are two solutions for this. First, narrowing the topic further will cut down on the amount of information that results. Narrowing the topic further will also make the search results more relevant. For instance, if you are interested in Shona folklore in Zimbabwe, adding the word "folklore" to your search will narrow Google's results to just over 32,000 sites; this number is still too many, but it is a considerable improvement over the initial 1.5 million!

Second, trying different search engines can help you identify relevant results a bit better. For instance, take a look at the results for Yandex.com. It has considerably fewer site results (110,000) to start. This lower number is a result of its search algorithms that try to provide more relevant information and of the geographical area it is trying to serve, which is Russia and other Central and Eastern European countries. Second, as noted, its search results are much more relevant than many of the other websites. Its first hit is titled "The History of Shona Tribe of Zimbabwe" and is from a website located directly in Zimbabwe. The rest of the results are relevant to the cultural background of the Shona people, such as music, language, and art.

Similarly, if you look at the results for Yippy.com, you'll see something extremely different about the search results. The number of results returned is again much more narrow. Yippy.com is trying to take advantage of advances in "big data" analysis—looking for patterns in large amounts of data. What better place to do that than on the Internet? What makes Yippy.com interesting and useful is that it is making a concerted effort to categorize the information into broad areas that will help narrow your search. Yippy.com refers to these as subject "clouds." If you are interested in Shona folklore, then you can click on one of those cloud links, such as the Shona Bible or Culture, to significantly narrow down the results to just a few sites. These types of search engines are still in development (as is "big data" science itself), but they are certainly on the cutting edge of how information gets categorized and made more accessible and relevant to students doing research. Still, it is not always immediately clear which search engine you may want to use. Give yourself some time to try different search engines.

Can You Google That?

Developers have created many search engines. The Search Engine List catalogs both general search engines and those that are more topic-specific. Despite a long list of search engines, Google is the most dominant and perhaps one of the most innovative. But even Google's general search engine can be a problem, as it does not sort information for you nor does it help you narrow your subject down to something manageable. This problem can be overcome by two of Google's tools (among the many they have developed): Google's advanced search engine and Google Scholar. Google's advanced search engine is shown in Figure 5.6 and can be found at https://www.google.com/advanced_search.

Notice first that you have many options for narrowing down your search. These can be quite useful in the Internet's information overload world. We'll use as our example one of the most common topics you will encounter in introductory psychology courses, the controversial Stanford Prison Experiment conducted by Philip Zimbardo more than four decades ago. We will leave

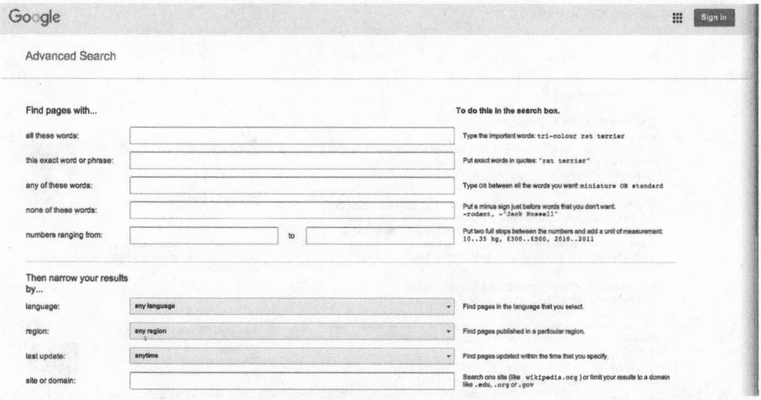

FIGURE 5.6 Google's Advanced Search Engine

the details of the experiment to your psychology professor, but we will start your inquiry here. Let's say that you need to do some research on how the Stanford Prison Experiment is used in psychology classes, but your professor wants only the most recent information—within the past four years. If you do a basic search for the Stanford Prison Experiment (Figure 5.7), you will find a common problem. With the release of the movie *The Stanford Prison Experiment* (2015), the Internet seems clogged with references to the movie rather than anything useful for your research.

This problem is a perfect example of how Google's advanced search tools can help. If we add a few conditions to the search, we can improve the results. First, let's get more specific with our keywords and add in the teaching element your professor wants. Then let's keep out anything related to the movie, so we tell Google to leave out "reviews," "film," and "movie" as terms within webpages to discard from the search results. Finally, your professor wanted only information from the past four years; so we restrict the dates of the information to 2013–2016. We now see results (Figure 5.8 and Figure 5.9) that begin to get to some useful information for you.

Quite a few results still appear, but the relevance of the search results is more in line with what you were hoping for. Notice also the search string and the operands needed in the search string to get these results. Many search engines would need you to know these operands to get the results you just got. Google has simplified that process nicely so that you do not need a cheat sheet of operands to limit your searches.

The second Google tool that can help you tremendously in your research is Google Scholar. Google Scholar is a research-specific search engine that

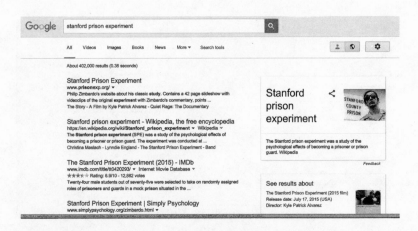

FIGURE 5.7 Google Search Results—Stanford Prison Experiment

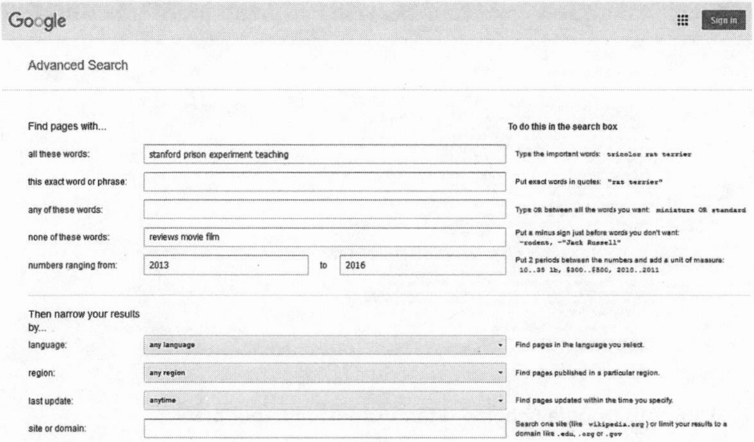

FIGURE 5.8 Google Advanced Search—Stanford Prison Experiment

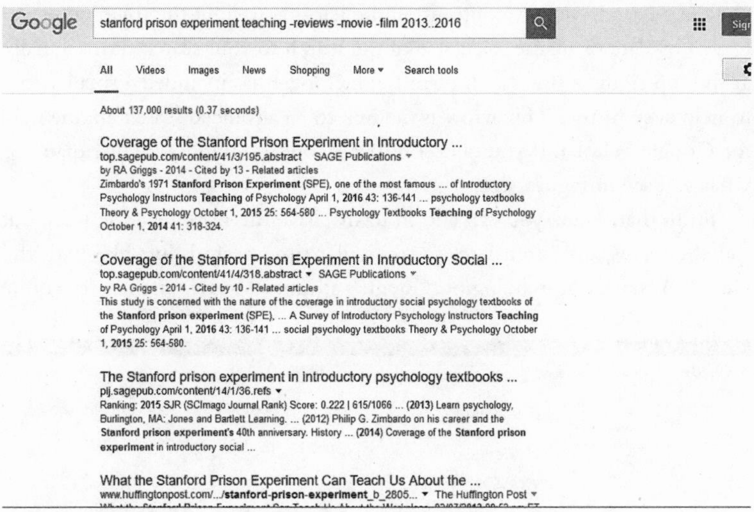

FIGURE 5.9 Google Advanced Search Results—Stanford Prison Experiment

indexes mostly authoritative research (again, we will discuss this issue a bit later). If we go back to our Stanford Prison Experiment example and type in the basic phrase "Stanford Prison Experiment" in the search field, we get the results in Figure 5.10.

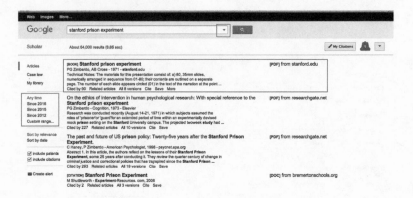

FIGURE 5.10 Google Scholar—Stanford Prison Experiment

There are three things to notice from the results. First, the results are much more specific and quite useful overall. Notice that the first result is the original *Stanford Prison Experiment* book, which is linked to an easily downloadable PDF file. Second, you have options on the left side to limit the time frame and to sort by date or by the relevance of the search to your search terms. Finally, at the top right in the search term field, Google has included a small arrow to help even further. This arrow is the link to an advanced search engine field for Google Scholar. If you click on that arrow, the window will expand to what you see in Figure 5.11.

From that menu, you can add in terms, have the search engine leave out specific terms, and limit dates to particular time periods just like with the Google advanced search engine. Google's advanced search engines save quite

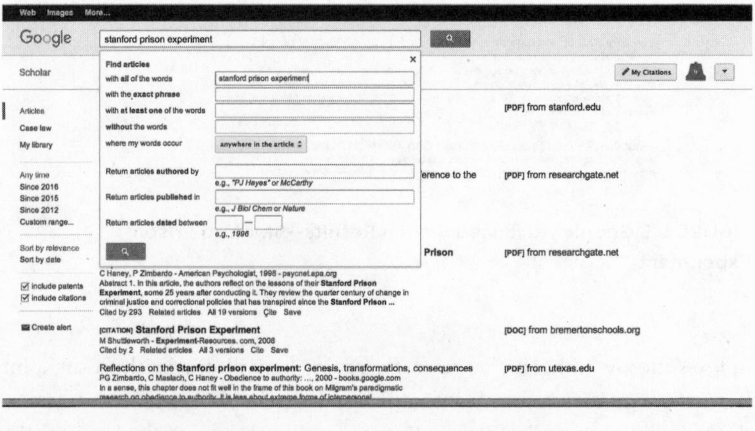

FIGURE 5.11 Google Scholar Advanced Search

a bit of time. Most advice regarding Internet search engines revolves around learning the long list of search operands (Boolean operators) that many search engines use to limit searches; Google's advanced search interface eliminates much of the need to remember these operands.

We want to reiterate one key piece of advice here—have good keywords for your search. Think of alternative ways to search for your topic and think of terms that can expand or narrow your search. With the advent of research on "big data" and "smart data" (finding patterns in large databases), Internet searches will become more sophisticated and responsive to the user's needs, and keyword searches are going to be even more important to narrow your focus.

A couple of words of caution should be added regarding your Internet searches. Be careful and be aware of any unusual file downloads or activities in websites. You do not want to inadvertently download a virus that can destroy your work or your computer. Routinely perform a virus scan of your computer so that you can stay ahead of this problem. Also, keep a backup of your information. With backup options that range from portable flash drives to cloud storage systems like iCloud, Amazon Drive, Google Drive (yes, more cool tools from Google), and Dropbox, there are no more plausible excuses for "computer problems" that destroyed your information and files.

A cloud storage system (many offer a limited amount of space for free or at very low rates) allows you to securely back up your information and generally to access it from any computer location in the world. Some colleges and universities have contracts with cloud services or have their own cloud service for students. Check with the computer and information technology center at your institution to see if they offer this type of service. It is good to back up your research work on these cloud systems, but still use caution before uploading personal information or anything you don't want to appear on the Internet. While these are generally good in terms of security, you don't want to take chances with lots of personal information or pictures in case these systems are breached by hackers. Sign up for one of these services and have peace of mind that all your research is backed up at least once, if not multiple times.

How Authoritative Are Your Sources?

The effectiveness of your research may depend upon how well you use three types of evidence: the first two are fairly standard—facts and logical deductions drawn from facts—while the third, expert opinion, has become a third kind of evidence for many researchers. Your research will probably draw upon all three of them (Gaston & Smith, 1988).

Facts are verifiable observations of some kind. People of similar mental, intellectual, and physical skills, who observe the same thing, should report similar findings on some event. Objective data produced by qualified people can provide evidence for some arguments or propositions. However, having the facts as evidence does not always settle the question as to whether the evidence is significant or sufficient to make the argument for you (Gaston & Smith, 1988, pp. 28–29). You need to be able to convince your audience that this is the case.

Facts often do not stand by themselves. It is up to you as the researcher to add context to the facts by drawing logical deductions and conclusions. This process follows a logical progression: the facts establish a claim to be made, the claim then fits with other evidence that fits a pattern, the pattern then becomes the preponderance of the evidence for your conclusion (Gaston & Smith, 1988, p. 29). In this sense, you are providing a plausible interpretation and context to the facts you have uncovered. An analogy can be made to solving a crime: the bits of evidence begin to tell a story that leads to the preponderance of the evidence pointing to the guilty person or persons. The idea is to build a logically plausible case for understanding the phenomena you are examining.

If we go back to our death penalty case from earlier, we can add some additional issues for the research. Your professor wants you to do a project that examines whether the death penalty is a deterrent to murder. After doing the appropriate searches in the database and on the Internet, you find three facts to begin building your argument: (a) states with the death penalty have higher murder rates than states without it, (b) more than 80 per cent of polled criminologists believe that existing research fails to support a deterrence justification for the death penalty, (c) states that have the death penalty do not have lower rates of murder for police officers (these data-based arguments can be found at the Death Penalty Focus website: http://deathpenalty.org). By themselves, the data do not represent a solid public policy argument against the death penalty. Why? There are plausible alternative explanations for each of these bits of evidence. States with the death penalty that have higher murder rates than states without it may have other characteristics that cause them to have higher murder rates: high drug use, gangs, youth crime, increased availability of guns, poverty, and unemployment are all factors that contribute to higher crime. However, as you start to bring these points of data together into a logical story about what the death penalty should do as a deterrent, the argument becomes stronger, though maybe not conclusive, that the death penalty does not act as a deterrent to crime.

Expert opinion gets us to the wider issue of how authoritative your research is. As we discussed earlier, the democratization of information, in terms of both access and production, has produced a mountain of information on many subjects. One of the important questions everyone has to face is: How authoritative is that information? Your professors will be critical of your sources, particularly if they seem questionable in terms of how authoritative they are. But in the universe of information, how can you tell if your information and sources are "authoritative," and what does that mean? These questions are not easy ones to answer; if they were, we wouldn't be discussing them here. But who qualifies as an "expert" or as being "authoritative" is also a question that does not have an easy answer, especially if the research you are reading is advocating ideas against the conventional wisdom or against a generally or popularly accepted idea. There is no absolute, foolproof way to determine whether someone is an expert. Again, we can determine this by identifying whether someone does or does not have the appropriate experience or qualifications to speak or write on a particular subject. That being said, Gaston and Smith provide some suggestions for making a distinction between good sources and bad sources (Gaston & Smith, 1988, pp. 30–33).

Distinguishing Authoritative Sources
✓ Always prefer acknowledged sources to self-proclaimed ones
✓ Make sure the experts are discussing their area of expertise
✓ Give first-hand accounts preference over second-hand ones
✓ Prefer unbiased research to research that comes from a particular argument or perspective
✓ Information that has stood the test of time and is still being cited is usually credible
✓ Give preference to research that is published in professional outlets

Always prefer acknowledged sources to self-proclaimed ones. What is the person's reputation within their field? Is their research published and cited? These people are acknowledged as experts in their field by other experts and researchers through a peer review process that validates the research and conclusions the authors present. There are literally hundreds of subject journals in the social sciences, and your reference librarian can help you isolate appropriate ones for your topic or idea.

Make sure the experts are discussing their area of expertise. The researchers should not be extending beyond their area of expertise into a field in which they have no background or training in doing research. Would you trust a political scientist to provide commentary and advice on neurosurgery? We hope not.

Give first-hand accounts preference over second-hand ones. People have a much different perspective on events they witnessed than do people who are reporting on them second-hand. That does not mean that second-hand accounts are useless, but their facts should be examined carefully.

Prefer unbiased research to research that comes from a particular argument or perspective. There are times when you want research from a particular perspective. However, if you are trying to examine a topic from an objective perspective, then you want to see research that is also objective. Subjective research can be useful, but you must recognize that it is starting from a particular viewpoint. Unbiased research does not make its conclusions up front. And sources matter—would you give more credibility to a report on smoking and cancer from tobacco manufacturers or from a report by the Centers for Disease Control? Bias should not be confused with conclusions reached from the research. If the researcher has come to particular conclusions based on an appropriate study she or he has conducted, then the conclusion is not biased, assuming the researcher conducted the study properly.

Information that has stood the test of time and is still being cited is usually credible. At the same time, you want to be aware that old information can be outdated. Make sure you use the most recent information when it is appropriate. Older research needs to be evaluated for its current validity. If current studies cite the older research, you know it is still valid. This is important; otherwise, we would still say that the sun revolves around the earth!

Give preference to research that is published in professional outlets. These may include known publishers or peer-reviewed journals instead of self-published studies or in-house reports. Publishers of books and journals usually follow a peer review process ensuring that experts or people familiar with the topic have examined the book or research article for appropriate research protocols, clarity of argument, and overall research quality.

To summarize, the central issues in finding authoritative sources are the transparency of information and whether research has followed a substantial review process. These are the key concerns when dealing with a popular website that some professors love and some professors loathe: Wikipedia. Most professors will not, and probably should not, let you cite it in a research paper. Why? As Cornell University's Digital Literacy Resource (n.d.) points out, Wikipedia is an encyclopedia of general knowledge, and most professors are looking beyond basic knowledge for any topic you are examining. Wikipedia is also an open source document that allows people to edit the entries at will. There is no real peer review process to guarantee the authoritativeness of the research, and there is no real way to know who has written or edited the entries. Thus, you and your professor should be extremely skeptical of Wikipedia as an authoritative source.

What to Do with Your Information: Writing, Organizing, and Common Mistakes

After your library and online sources are in hand, it is up to you to start making sense of all the materials that you have collected. Some forethought and organization will be useful here, as you need to have a vision for what this finished project will look like and a method for getting it done. The first thing you want to think about is the environment in which you will be writing and the ways that we sometimes self-sabotage when we begin writing.

Multitasking: Something We Are Horrible at Doing

We have grown up in an age of information and computer technology that makes each of us believe that we can multitask and do all of those tasks well. Let's dispense with the illusion that we can multitask and think instead about some ideas and habits that will serve to move your project forward efficiently and successfully (so you get the grades that you want or need).

To break the multitasking mentality, think about doing one specific task at a time. We cannot count the times we have seen students in libraries or have had conversations with students who are working on projects that just don't seem to move forward. We generally ask our students, "What approach do you take in writing? What is it like when you write?" The responses we receive are pretty typical. "Well, I have my music on and all my articles and books in front of me. Sometimes the TV is on and then I start trying to type but the ideas don't seem to come to me." The general problem is that there is too much going on here. Writing does not come naturally, and it takes time to do it well. For this reason alone, projects need to have early and frequent attention.

There are several things that sabotage your effort here. Loud music, where you are singing along to lyrics while thinking your fans are cheering for you, is not going to let you focus. In fact, high intensity music creates an Attention Drainage Effect on students and adversely affects the ability to perform tasks and to concentrate on them (Chou, 2010). Subtle or quiet music can sometimes reinforce concentration on the task at hand, but it should be background music and nothing you particularly notice.

Another set of huge distractions is also electronic: televisions, cell phones, and email. While television is a visual distraction, cell phones and email can be really problematic in other ways. They create a sense of urgency to return messages constantly. Most of the time there is no real "emergency" to which you must respond instantaneously. While these tools are an integral part of your life, they are also your biggest distractions. Be more selfish with your time. You and your family may be paying thousands of dollars for an education, and you should get the most out of it. Think about turning off your cell phone and putting it in your backpack. Out of sight, out of mind. People can leave you a message and you can check your phone every couple of hours.

The next set of distractions may surprise you a bit, given they are such an important part of getting work done. Your critical sources of information—computers, books, and articles—can distract you from getting your writing done. This may seem counterintuitive, but all these things can act as barriers to project completion. Students who are pressed for time will often bypass some basic steps, sit at a desk with a stack of books, and just start typing. This process may be the most dangerous thing you can do with projects. Bad habits develop out of shortcuts, and big mistakes often come from bad habits.

Let's examine this scenario. As you are typing words directly into a computer with little thought going into the process, you are, in fact, trying to do too many things at one time. Think about it—students who do this are trying to do their research, to read through their books and articles, to write their summaries, to type, and often to edit for grammar and organization—all at the same time! The usual outcome of this scenario is a complete mess that requires more work to fix than if you had followed a systematic approach. In the worst case (as we have seen so many times), such sloppiness in the writing process can lead to improper source citation and charges of research misconduct and plagiarism. So how do you work at your most efficient level? You need to have a specific, systematic process that can be adapted for all your projects.

Steps to Writing Efficiently
- ✓ Extract information from your sources and organize it
- ✓ Outline a plan for your writing
- ✓ Write
- ✓ Edit your project

Extracting Information

The first thing that needs attention is your sources. You need to cull information from your sources and have that information easily organized so that it can be referenced. You should begin by reading each of your sources for useful points and information related to your topic. Then organize this information so that you can access it as you write your paper. There are two ways to do this, and either of them can be a great way to organize material. The first is an old, tried and true method for dealing with information: index cards. For each source, create a card that has the following information:

- *The bibliographic reference information at the top of the card.* You will need this for documenting your sources and for your bibliography anyway, so it is best to start with this information.
- *Main finding of the research.* In no more than three sentences, what is the main finding or the main argument of the research?
- *Logical argument and material support that underpins the main finding.* Document and highlight the important points the author used to get to their main idea and the page numbers noted in the source. Do this by summarizing the author's main argument or issue, and only quote information that cannot be rephrased or makes a very specific point you need to make in the drafting of the paper. By avoiding most direct quotations, you will avoid mistakes that can lead to plagiarism and accusations of improper research procedures. You will still need to cite where you got the idea from, but you will not need to add specific quotes to the paper.

This same process can be done in several different ways. Some people prefer using index cards because it forces them to limit the number of points needed to summarize the article. Others like to do this with a word processing program because they are used to typing everything on their computer. Some like to use reference management or bibliographic software to help them document and take notes on their sources. Bibliographic software has come a long way in recent years. Early editions of some software packages did not provide much of an advantage over using a word processor or an index card. In fact, they were clunky enough to make the process more of a burden. Today, advances in how software has been integrated into online search results and the ability to download references from databases makes doing this kind of documentation much easier than with previous software editions.

Bibliographic Software

Three bibliographic software packages to consider are Endnote, RefWorks, and Zotero. Endnote and RefWorks are standard at most colleges and universities. Students can usually buy a copy of Endnote through their bookstore, or it may be free through a licensing agreement with your library or information technology center. RefWorks is an online, Internet-based program. You can purchase a subscription online, or it also may be available through your university or college. Zotero is free and integrates into your web browser so that you can capture citation information directly from web pages! It is this feature that distinguishes Zotero from any other bibliographic software package currently on the market. Zotero is able to detect reference material on thousands of websites so that all you have to do is click a button to download the bibliographic information for the reference into Zotero's management program. You can then cite this information as you type your paper and generate your bibliography at the end of your paper with a few clicks of some buttons. Zotero has the ability to do this for library databases such as JSTOR and EBSCO and for Google Scholar searches and regular webpages. To use this feature, you generally need Firefox, Chrome, or Safari as your browser, and you need to install the Zotero connector (explained in their documentation), but it can be a major time saver.

Each professor you encounter may want a certain citation format. All you need to do to accommodate that request is specify the citation format in Endnote, RefWorks, or Zotero and you are set to go. That ability, by itself, is a time saver when writing. Each of these programs also allows you to take and store notes and files with each of the citations you have in the software. So while you are collecting your sources, you can take notes right in the reference and attach your PDF and Word document files to the citations. Again, this is another way of organizing your notes so that everything is right in front of you when you begin writing. You should read the webpages for these software packages and talk to your reference librarian to determine which one will work best for you.

Once you decide the method by which you will take notes, you need to decide what to document. What important points should be noted in your sources? This process goes back to a fundamental issue: what is your research about? Notes should not be taken only within the context of the article, but also in the wider context of what your research question or project focus is. Each note that you take from your sources should be related to making an argument or a specific point about your research topic. Researchers often write in this same way, focusing on specific arguments or points about their topics.

Researchers begin articles or a book with an outline that is reflected in the headings and subheadings. Use those to your advantage to divide the research into logically connected sections. Then summarize the most important points that you need for understanding your research question or topic. Once you do this, define key terminology that you think you will need. Again, try to avoid copying long quotes, and quote only things that are very specific. If you are using bibliographic software for this, resist the temptation to just cut and paste into the summary fields of the citation; this is where there is often a danger of inadvertently plagiarizing. Think about what the author is saying and then rephrase the research into your own words.

Suggestions for Avoiding Plagiarism
Plagiarism is taking someone else's ideas without attribution. It is a form of academic theft. The problem has become so endemic on campuses that many

universities and colleges have adopted Internet software to detect plagiarism in students' and professors' research. To be fair, it does not just afflict student research; many professors have suffered the consequences of falsifying research or plagiarizing (see, for instance, the Retraction Watch website, which tracks the retraction of scientific research for reasons of research misconduct). The penalties for students can be severe, including failing assignments, failing classes, being placed on academic probation, and even being expelled from the university or college. For researchers, the consequences can be the loss of their income, job, grants, and reputation. It is easy to fall into a situation, intended or not, where you have plagiarized someone's research or information.

Regardless of the reason, *you* are responsible for what you produce, and *there is no acceptable excuse for plagiarism.* The consequences of plagiarism often are much greater than the consequences for turning in a late paper. Think about the consequences before you do something that can be avoided. Here are some ways to avoid plagiarism from Harvard College's Writing Program and The Writing Center @ The University of Wisconsin–Madison.

Avoiding Plagiarism
- ✓ Make sure you track your sources
- ✓ Budget your time
- ✓ Avoid cutting and pasting from electronic sources
- ✓ Keep documents separate
- ✓ Paraphrase carefully when you are writing your content
- ✓ Do not wait until the end of the project to compile your citations
- ✓ Keep all of your research information and sources
- ✓ Cite when you are unsure

Make sure you track your sources. Organize your electronic sources either in a folder on your computer or with bibliographic software. Log complete website URL information and the date that you accessed it. You should either print your websites or save them as PDF files that you can store in your folder or bibliographic software.

Budget your time. Research is time-consuming, and we always tend to *underestimate* the amount of time it takes to complete it. Taking shortcuts because you are running out of time is probably one of the main reasons plagiarism occurs. Doing projects at the last moment when you are under stress, tired, and have other assignments to do can create a careless environment.

Avoid cutting and pasting from electronic sources. Take notes on index cards or in bibliographic software, but never cut and paste into electronic documents of any kind. If you are typing your notes in a word processor, keep each source in a separate file with the proper citation information and page numbers. If you are using bibliographic software for your notes, make sure you log in the date of your notes and the page numbers where your information came from in the research.

Keep documents separate. Do not blend or mix your project draft, your sources, and the notes for your sources together. Keep them in separate folders and do not keep them open all at once.

Paraphrase carefully when you are writing your content. Putting ideas and arguments in your own words will get you thinking about why you are using the source. At the same time, you *do not want to string together a bunch of paraphrased sources*; remember, this is your research project and your professor is looking for an original piece of research and thought from *you*. Make sure you cite paraphrased elements of your project appropriately and that you track those citations in your notes.

Do not wait until the end of the project to compile your citations. You will never remember every place where you have quoted or paraphrased in the project. If you are quoting or paraphrasing, make sure that you cite the information immediately so you do not forget. Make sure direct quotes are set off with quotation marks to indicate that these are not your words. Likewise, each discipline has its own way of citing information (there are literally hundreds of citation formats that are used); make sure you understand which citation format your professor prefers for your research. Few things are more tedious than having to reformat all your citations to comply with your professor's instructions.

Keep all of your research information and sources. Even after you have turned in your project, SAVE EVERYTHING. If a question ever arises about your research, you will be able to go back and show your professor where you got information and how you progressed through your project. Being able to do this will strengthen your credibility during a period when your professor may be looking at you and your research with some skepticism.

Cite when you are unsure. In general, if you are unsure if you have to cite something, the safest thing is to ask your professor or reference librarian. If they are unavailable during your all-nighter, then cite it to be safe.

What to Cite in Your Research
- ✓ Specific words or phrases used by an author
- ✓ Information that is not common knowledge
- ✓ Ideas

Specific words or phrases used by an author. You need quotation marks for these citations, and you should attribute them appropriately. When using direct quotes you must also include the specific page number in the citation.

Information that is not common knowledge. Common knowledge may be information that is in the public domain, such as generally accepted dates of events. If you can find the information in several general information sources or encyclopedias, it is safe to say it is common knowledge. Specific data, facts, or figures should be cited.

Ideas. Specific researchers' ideas must be cited; these may include research points, conclusions drawn from information, a definition, or a method or theory.

Outlining a Plan for Your Writing

By the time you are done reading your sources and taking notes on them, you will probably have a sense of what your project may look like. Before you start writing, however, you still want to have a roadmap, and the best way to do this is to outline your project. This outline does not have to be extensive or extremely detailed. The purpose of developing an outline is to see how the main points of your project are coming together and whether they make logical sense within the scope of the thesis or research question. Your outline could be a simple two-level topical outline, though the more levels of detail you can add, the easier it will be to write. If we go back to the death penalty deterrence project, an outline for that project might look like this:

Is the Death Penalty an Effective Deterrent to Violent Crime?

Thesis: The death penalty does not serve as an effective deterrent to violent crime.

I. Introduction
   a. Lead-in to describe the issue
   b. Your thesis: The death penalty does not serve as an effective deterrent to violent crime.
II. Evidence favoring the deterrence argument
   a. Supporters of the deterrence argument
   b. Evidence for the deterrence argument
   c. Strengths and weaknesses of the evidence for the deterrence argument
III. Evidence against the deterrence argument
   a. Opponents of the death penalty
   b. Evidence against the deterrence argument
   c. Strengths and weaknesses of the evidence against the deterrence argument

IV. Conclusion
    a. Summarize main points
        1. Supporters
        2. Opponents
    b. Highlight thesis and evidence for the thesis

Now print the outline, pin it up next to your desk, and keep your focus on it! The idea is to always have a roadmap so that your paper is being written with organization of thought. You want your paper to have some flow and logic to it; by referring to that map, your paper will keep its organization. If your outline does not make sense to you, you can easily restructure it right away instead of in the middle of a 20-page project. Organized research and an organized presentation of it can be the difference between that A paper and that B paper.

Writing Your Project

Once you have the outline and your vision for the paper, the process for writing it can begin. If you have dedicated the time to a research project, the best thing that you can do to develop good writing skills is to get away from your computer. This sounds almost deranged in the information technology age. You need your computer! You can't live without your computer! Actually, you can, and there are times that you should. The objective, with time, is to get you to focus on the actual process of writing. To do that, you need to focus on writing and not on the mechanics of software issues, formatting, and all the associated problems of modern computers. Pick up a pencil and a big writing tablet and start writing based on your outline. Don't worry about grammar and spelling for the time being—this will be addressed later. Follow your outline and keep writing and keep pushing. Write as quickly as you can just to get something on the paper, using the notes you created from your resources. If the notes are in bibliographic software, open the program so you can see your references, but do not type in a word processing program. Let the ideas and thoughts go from your brain directly to your paper.

Which section you decide to tackle first often does not matter. But we do have one suggestion: write the introduction and conclusion last. Think of it this way: these are sections that are based on the body of the research project. If you haven't written the body of the project, then what are you going to say to introduce or to conclude the project? We can waste valuable writing time trying to figure out what to say in the introduction, when in fact we haven't written anything that is going to help us with figuring that out.

It is also useful to understand what the introduction and conclusion should do. There really is no consensus on what an introduction should do for your research project. This depends on what the project is supposed to do. Is the project supposed to convince the reader of something? Is it supposed to be an investigation to inform the reader? These ideas need to be integrated into the introduction. Aside from what the project should be doing, you should be telling your reader why your research is important—grab your reader's attention here. Introduce your research question and explain why it is important. What makes your research topic important or special? It may be the case that from a bigger, general perspective, you are not able to link your topic to an important aspect that will affect someone's life. It is probably difficult to link metaphors in West African folklore to an immediate issue or concern to someone's day-to-day life. Have you provided a new way to interpret some particular metaphors in folklore that could be useful to researchers? Have you compared methods for investigating a phenomenon and found one is better than other methods? It is critical to remember that the importance of a topic may be discipline-specific and not necessarily important to everyone on the planet at some given time. If that is the case, then you want to frame your introduction as something that is discipline- or topic-specific.

The conclusion to your project has some of the same function that the introduction has. What else you put into the conclusion depends on the purpose of the paper. In most cases, you still want to highlight the importance of the research, as you did in the introduction. In doing so, you want to leave readers with the idea that what they just read has some significance and that they have an answer to the basic question: "Why should I care?" The last thing you want is for someone to think "So what?" when they finish your paper. Thus, you want to bring out the significant points, results, or even unexpected results. Finally, what are the implications for your project and what do you think needs to be done in future research on the topic? These questions may be appropriate to address in your conclusion, depending upon the nature of the paper and the subject matter.

Editing Your Project

When your writing is done, you can then open your word processing program. Make sure you have set all the various margins and font requirements that your professor may have given in the instructions for the paper. Most papers should have their type sized at 12 points in a standard font such as Times New Roman or Arial. Don't get too fancy or cute with font choices and other ways to manipulate page length—most of your professors have gone through this and know as many secrets to doing these things as you do. Now, begin to type from the handwritten manuscript. By doing this, you break down the writing process so that you are not doing everything all at once. You can now type and edit your manuscript without necessarily worrying about content as you type. All you are doing is typing and doing large edits for grammar and spelling. This process will help you move quickly through the manuscript that you have handwritten. While at first this may seem like a big waste of time, it turns out that you will spend only a little more time doing this and your paper will be better written because of the process.

Once you are done typing and doing the first edits on the manuscript, you have one other key step to go through. You should now print the project and do two final edits. The first is for technical elements of grammar and punctuation. Visit your university's, or college's writing center or its website to see if there is a cheat sheet for common grammatical and writing issues. If there isn't, there are plenty of websites that can help deal with common grammatical and writing problems associated with writing research papers.

The second edit will be a bit unusual. Starting from the title page through to your conclusion, read the project out loud. (Yes, make sure there are no roommates around so you don't sound like you have turned your apartment into a big lecture hall.) Here's why: if you read something aloud and it doesn't sound right, then, most often, it is not right. Your ears will catch mistakes that your probably very tired eyes will not be able to catch. Let your ears do your final edits for you. Many mistakes can be caught this way. Ideally, at this point you still have time before you have to turn in the project. If so, put the project away for a few hours (maybe a couple of days) and then go back to read it aloud one more time.

Research and Crunch Time

Finally, if you find yourself in a time crunch (and all of us eventually do), and you do not feel you can manage a more thorough approach to your project, then by all means open the word processor and start typing instead of handwriting your first draft. Realistically this will happen to you, though it should be less frequent as you move through your career, gaining experience from your mistakes and practicing the points we have made here. Try to create and follow an outline so that you can build structure into the paper as you are working through it. But follow the same mental approach for handwriting your manuscript. Write for content first. Do not use your backspace key; do not allow your software to complain about misspelled words or grammatical structure. Once you have written the entire manuscript, start at the beginning of the paper and do the major edits for grammar and spelling. Then print the manuscript and do the two edits described above. This process is not the ideal scenario and you are going to be more susceptible to errors, but it will get you through the paper.

Important Points to Remember

✓ Be sure to understand your professor's expectations before beginning your research process
✓ Subject/resource librarians are your friends—be sure to know all the ways they can help you find information and conduct research
✓ Take the time to learn how to research databases effectively and efficiently
✓ When conducting Internet searches, understand how different search engines generate results and then choose your search engine wisely
✓ Know how to judge the reliability of sources
✓ When writing, reduce distractions and avoid multitasking
✓ Have a writing plan and stick with it
✓ Remember that writing is a process with multiple steps. Make sure you have time for each one
✓ Understand plagiarism and avoid it at all costs
✓ And, it bears repeating, LIBRARIANS ARE YOUR FRIENDS!

Bibliography

Chou, P. T.-M. (2010). Attention drainage effect: How background music effects concentration in Taiwanese college students. *Journal of the Scholarship of Teaching and Learning, 10*(1), 36–46.

Cornell University Digital Literacy Resource. (n.d.). Digital literacy resource—A guide to doing research online—Using Wikipedia. Retrieved from http://digitalliteracy.cornell.edu/tutorial/dpl3222.html

Death Penalty Focus. (n.d.). Deterrence. Retrieved from http://deathpenalty.org

Gaston, T. E., & Smith, B. H. (1988). *The research paper: A common-sense approach.* Englewood Cliffs, NJ: Prentice-Hall.

Harvard College Writing Program. (n.d.). Harvard guide to using sources: How to avoid plagiarism. Retrieved from http://isites.harvard.edu/icb/icb.do?keyword=k70847&pageid=icb.page342057

Magi, T. J., & Mardeusz, P. E. (2013). Why some students continue to value individual, face-to-face research consultations in a technology-rich world. *College & Research Libraries, 74*(6), 605–18. http://dx.doi.org/10.5860/crl12-363

Purdue OWL. (n.d.). Conducting primary research. Retrieved from https://owl.
    english.purdue.edu/owl/resource/559/01/

The Writing Center @ the University of Wisconsin–Madison. (n.d.). Avoiding
    plagiarism: Quoting and paraphrasing. Retrieved from https://writing.wisc.edu/
    Handbook/QPA_plagiarism.html

Woetzel, D. (n.d.). Research guides: Research @ Reynolds Library: 4 b.
    Online search strategies. Retrieved from http://libguides.reynolds.edu/c.
    php?g=143583&p=939839

Web Links

No, we still have not received any money for mentioning these.
We are open for suggestions on this idea.

Academic Search Premier | Scholarly Research Database | EBSCO: https://www.
    ebscohost.com/academic/academic-search-premier

Amazon Cloud: https://www.amazon.com/clouddrive/home

American Sociological Association: Data Resources on Sociology as a Profession:
    http://www.asanet.org/research/data_resources.cfm

Dropbox: https://www.dropbox.com

EndNote: http://endnote.com/

GenderWatch: http://www.proquest.com/products-services/genderwatch.html

Google Drive: https://www.google.com/drive/

Google Scholar: https://scholar.google.com/

iCloud: https://www.icloud.com/

Inter-university Consortium for Political & Social Research (ICPSR): http://www.
    icpsr.umich.edu/index.html

LexisNexis Academic & Library Solutions: http://www.lexisnexis.com/hottopics/
    lnacademic/

Lynda.com: https://www.lynda.com/

Microsoft Office Suite: http://www.microsoftstore.com/store/msusa/en_US/cat/
    All-Office/categoryID.69403900

Minitab: https://www.minitab.com/en-us/

ProQuest—Databases: http://www.proquest.com/libraries/academic/databases

ProQuest History Vault: The Black Freedom Struggle in the 20th Century: http://
    proquest.libguides.com/historyvault/bfsfed

PubMed—NCBI: http://www.ncbi.nlm.nih.gov/pubmed

The R Project for Statistical Computing: https://www.r-project.org/

RefWorks: http://www.refworks.com/refworks

Registry of Research Data Repositories: http://www.re3data.org/

SPSS: http://www.ibm.com/analytics/us/en/technology/spss/

Stata: http://www.stata.com/

Statistics Canada: http://www.statcan.gc.ca/eng/start

Stat/Transfer Data Conversion Software: http://www.stattransfer.com/

UNdata: http://data.un.org/

US Government's Open Data Site: https://www.data.gov/

Westlaw: http://legalsolutions.thomsonreuters.com/law-products/westlaw-legal-research/

World Bank World Development Indicators: http://data.worldbank.org/products/wdi

Zotero: https://www.zotero.org/

INDEX